The Asian Cookbook

The Asian Cookbook

p

This is a Parragon Publishing Book

This edition published in 2006

Parragon Publishing
Queen Street House
4 Queen Street
Bath BA1 1HE, UK

Copyright © Parragon Books Ltd 2005

ISBN: 1-40546-576-X

Printed in China

Produced by the Bridgewater Book Company Ltd

NOTES FOR THE READER

- This book uses imperial, metric, and US cup measurements. Follow the same units of measurement throughout; do not mix imperial and metric.

- All spoon measurements are level: teaspoons are assumed to be 5 ml, and tablespoons are assumed to be 15 ml.

- Unless otherwise stated, milk is assumed to be whole, eggs and individual vegetables such as potatoes are medium, and pepper is freshly ground black pepper.

- Recipes using raw or very lightly cooked eggs should be avoided by infants, the elderly, pregnant women, convalescents, and anyone suffering from an illness.

- Pregnant and breast-feeding women are advised to avoid eating peanuts and peanut products.

- The times given are an approximate guide only. Preparation times differ according to the techniques used by different people and the cooking times may also vary from those given.

Contents

Introduction

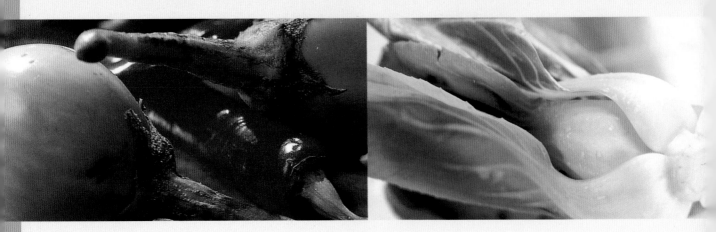

Introduction

8

Who can resist the unforgettable aromas and flavors of food from Asia? Tender morsels lovingly prepared, cooked with mouthwatering combinations of exotic spices, tantalize the taste buds and leave the palate longing for more. Asia is a place of many contrasts and cultures, and dramatic landscapes that are the source of many exciting foods, some well known outside of Asia, and some not.

This book is a celebration of some of the best of Asian cuisines, from the marvelous and unmistakable food of China, and the heady, fragrant dishes of India, to the beautifully prepared dishes of Thailand. Each of these countries can boast its own specialties that will impress and delight you.

The timeless food of China

Chinese cooking is time-honored and yet extremely practical. Since ancient times, cooks have enjoyed a flexibility in their cuisine that is unknown in many nations. Delicious meats, poultry, fish, and vegetables have been stir-fried with sauces and different combinations of flavorings, then paired with grains such as rice and noodles. During times of scarcity, cooks would skillfully make nutritious and satisfying meals out of very little, while during times of plenty or affluence, more luxurious ingredients could be added. In this way, Chinese cuisine merely adapted to the times rather than changed, retaining its basic philosophies and traditions.

Modern-day Chinese cooking can be divided into four distinct regions: north, east, south, and west. In the north of China in areas such as Beijing, the climate is dry, with harsh winters. In this northern territory, one of the staples is wheat flour, so you are much more likely to find noodles here than rice. Although Beijing and some parts of the north are close to the East China Sea, the cuisine in this region is less influenced by seafood and more by meat and poultry dishes, such as the

Peking Duck of the inland areas. It is also the source of Peking sauce, and Fu Yung, which is an egg sauce. Foreign trade brought many new ingredients to the north, and today local dishes include sesame seeds, walnuts, peas, cilantro, grapes, and garlic.

In eastern China, in the fertile valley of Shanghai and the surrounding areas, rice is widely used, and egg-fried rice originated here. Locally caught shellfish and fish from the Yangtze River feature widely on the menu. Also popular are duck, goose, pork, and cured ham, and common flavorings include honey, ginger, and rice wine, although stir-fried dishes are often flavored simply with soy sauce.

From the south of China comes the most famous style of cooking, which has become popular all over the world. Cantonese cooking is the style that is most familiar to Westerners, and from this region originated such popular dishes as dim sum, as well as sweet-and-sour sauces and spectacular seafood dishes.

In western China, in Sichuan and Hunan and surrounding areas, the cuisine is hot and spicy, with a liberal use of chilies. This region is much farther from the sea than the other areas, and its humidity has resulted in an abundance of preserved foods, especially those that have been pickled, salted, dried, or smoked. This area is also famed for its cured ham, which is known as Yunnan or Xuanwei ham.

Although the different regions of China vary greatly in terms of landscape and cuisine, stir-fries are popular throughout China, and their popularity has spread to the rest of the world. Stir-frying is a very healthy way to cook, since it requires only a small quantity of oil, and the cooking time is short. The best pan for stir-frying is a wok—a large, deep, bowl-shaped skillet. Woks are traditionally made with two small handles, but you can now buy ones with a single long handle, which many cooks prefer. You can also use a large skillet for stir-frying, but a wok is better, since it is easier to toss the food around a wok, and the heat is distributed more evenly because more food comes into contact with the hot bottom and sides of the wok.

Generally, you will not see any knives on a Chinese dinner table, because the food is cut by the cook in the kitchen before it is brought out to the table. Neither will you see salt and pepper pots: the Chinese believe that it is an insult to season your food after the cook has spent so much time and effort preparing it!

9

India—land of unforgettable flavors

Like China, India can be divided into four distinct culinary regions. Northern India, which encompasses the state of Punjab, among others, can be searingly hot at times and very cold at others. The cuisine that has developed here is therefore quite rich. This is the home of tandoori cooking. This region has produced many of the specialties that are familiar in the West, such as kormas and nan bread. Lamb is also popular here. Dishes are often flavored with garam masala, which is a blend of dry-roasted, ground spices.

In the east, where you will find the states of Orissa and West Bengal, the climate is hot, and humidity is high. Unlike the north, where bread is popular, rice is the favored grain food. Since this region is near to the Bay of Bengal, fish is very common, and coconuts and bananas are grown here. Tea is a very popular drink in India, and the eastern region is renowned for its Assam and Darjeeling teas.

In the south, including the states of Goa and Kerala, there is a lot more rainfall, and therefore an abundance of vegetables and beans. Here you will find delicious dishes, known as dal, made with lentils or other beans. The diet here is chiefly vegetarian, but there are also meat dishes. You will also find fiery vindaloos and seafood.

In western India, including the state of Gujarat, you will find an abundance of yogurt, buttermilk, and milk-based dishes. Pickles are popular here too. Mumbai (Bombay) on the western coast is where northern India meets the south, and here you can see a fusion of different ingredients. For example, both wheat and rice are staples. You will also find a wide variety of fish and shellfish dishes. Naturally, western India also has its share of fresh vegetables, and Gujarat carrot salad is a specialty here.

You do not need any special equipment to prepare delicious Indian food for yourself—most dishes can be cooked in one or more large pans on the stove. However, a mortar and pestle is useful for grinding spices.

India also has its own version of the wok: a two-handled pan known as a "balti" pan, or "karahi." Some Indians use it to prepare a kind of stir-fried curry, while others use it to prepare a meal of meat and vegetables, which is eaten from the pan itself. If you do not have a balti pan, use a large wok or large, deep skillet.

The exquisite food of Thailand

Thailand can be divided into three culinary regions: north, central, and south. In the north, which is far from the sea, popular dishes include vegetables, steamed rice, and chili sauces. Pork, sausages, chicken, and duck are also popular here.

In central Thailand, rice is the great staple, and vegetable soups and salads are very popular. Here you can also find Thai omelets, roasted beef or pork, and locally caught fish. This is also the home of Thai red curry. Food presentation is an art here, and has helped Thai cuisine become famous internationally.

In southern Thailand, in Bangkok and other southern regions, the cuisine is very hot and fiery: chilies are widely used in dishes. This is also the region nearest to the sea, so you will also find seafood on the menu.

Thai cooks use a marvelous range of herbs and spices, including garlic, galangal, chili, kaffir lime leaves, lemongrass, sweet basil, cumin, and turmeric, which lend an unmistakable flavor to a wide range of dishes.

To cook Thai food, you do not need any special equipment. If you buy a Chinese wok, you can use it to cook food from Thailand as well as China. Likewise, a mortar and pestle will serve you well for preparing ingredients.

As in China, you will not normally see any knives on the Thai table because the food is cut by the cook in the kitchen. Also, in Thailand all dishes are shared. The dishes will come out gradually, with diners helping themselves to each dish one spoonful at a time, so remember to leave some food on each dish for others!

Impressive meals in minutes

You can conjure up the aromas and flavors of Asia in your kitchen very quickly with the use of some basic pantry ingredients. Chinese egg noodles, basmati rice, and thin rice noodles are a must. Add to this a range of Asian spices and other staples such as lentils, soy sauce, Peking sauce, and Thai fish sauce. And buy fresh ingredients as and when necessary.

The recipes in this book are simple yet impressive, quick to make, and mouthwateringly delicious. They will delight and inspire everyone who tries them, and leave you amazed that they took so little time to prepare.

11

Basic Recipes

Thai red curry paste

1 tbsp coriander seeds
1 tbsp cumin seeds
2 tsp shrimp paste
12 dried or fresh red chilies, chopped
2 shallots, chopped
8 garlic cloves, chopped
1-inch/2.5-cm piece fresh
    galangal, chopped
2 lemongrass stalks (white parts
    only), chopped
4 kaffir lime leaves, chopped
2 tbsp chopped fresh cilantro root
grated zest of 1 lime
1 tsp black peppercorns

Dry-cook the coriander and cumin seeds in a skillet, stirring constantly, for 2–3 minutes, or until browned. Remove from the heat and grind to a powder using a pestle and mortar. Wrap the shrimp paste in a piece of foil and broil or dry-cook in a skillet for 2–3 minutes, turning once or twice. Put the ground spices, shrimp paste, and chilies in a food processor or blender and process until finely chopped.

Add the remaining ingredients and process again to a smooth paste, scraping down the sides as necessary.

Thai yellow curry paste

3 small, fresh, orange or yellow chilies,
    coarsely chopped
3 large garlic cloves, coarsely chopped
4 shallots, coarsely chopped
1 tbsp ground turmeric
1 tsp salt
12–15 black peppercorns
1 lemongrass stalk (white part only),
    coarsely chopped
1-inch/2.5-cm piece fresh
    gingerroot, chopped

Put all the ingredients in a food processor or blender and process to a thick paste, scraping down the sides as necessary.

Thai green curry paste

Follow the method for Thai red curry paste, but replace the chilies with 15 fresh, green, bird's eye chilies; use only 6 garlic cloves, and 6 kaffir lime leaves (not 4), and add 1 teaspoon of salt with the pepper.

Garlic and ginger paste

Blend together equal quantities of garlic and fresh gingerroot. Store in a sealed jar in the refrigerator for up to 3 weeks, or in the freezer for up to 1 month.

Thai magic paste

This recipe uses the trinity of Thai ingredients: a whole bulb of garlic, peeled and ground with a bunch of fresh cilantro leaves and roots and 1/4 cup white peppercorns. Keep in the refrigerator for 3–4 days or freeze in small amounts. This paste is also sold in jars.

Peking duck crêpes

These can be reheated in a steamer or microwave oven.

3 1/2 cups all-purpose flour, plus extra
   for dusting
pinch of salt
1 1/4 cups boiling water
2 tbsp cold water
1/2 tsp sesame oil

To make 30 crêpes, sift the flour and a pinch of salt into a bowl and slowly stir in the boiling water to make a thick dough. Add the cold water and sesame oil, then knead for 4 minutes, or until soft and smooth. Cover and let rest for 30 minutes.

Dust a counter with flour, divide the dough into two, and knead until smooth. Roll each portion into a log and divide into 15 balls. Roll each out to create a 6-inch/15-cm circle. Heat a dry skillet, then lower the heat. Place the crêpes in the pan and cook until little brown spots begin to appear. Flip over and cook for another 10 seconds.

Soft spring roll wrappers

The Chinese use both soft and hard wheat wrappers to enclose their spring rolls. Soft spring roll wrappers can be made at home.

generous 3 3/4 cups all-purpose flour
1 tsp salt
4 eggs, beaten
scant 2 cups cold water
6 tbsp vegetable oil

To make 20 soft spring roll wrappers, sift the flour into a bowl with the salt. Make a well in the center and stir in the beaten eggs. Slowly add the cold water, whisking to create a smooth and thick batter. Finally stir in the vegetable oil. To cook the crêpes, heat a small 6-inch/15-cm nonstick pan, drop a generous 3 tablespoons of the batter into the pan, and swirl. Cook until the edges peel away from the pan. Pile the crêpes on top of each other, then bring to the table for wrapping.

Soups, Appetizers, and Light Meals

SERVES 4–6

10 oz/280 g spareribs, cut into
small pieces

5 cups water

2 tomatoes, seeded and
coarsely chopped

3 thin slices fresh gingerroot

2½ cups bean sprouts

2 tsp salt

7 oz/200 g soft bean curd (drained
weight), cut into 1-inch/2.5-cm cubes

NGA CHOI DAU FU TONG
bean curd and bean sprout soup

Bring a pan of water to a boil and blanch the spareribs for about 30 seconds. Skim the water, remove the ribs, and set aside.

Bring the measured water to a boil and add the spareribs, tomatoes, and gingerroot. After 10 minutes, remove the tomato skins from the water. Add the bean sprouts and salt, cover, and simmer for 1 hour. Add the bean-curd cubes, simmer for another 2 minutes, then remove from the heat and serve.

SERVES 4–6

generous ⅓ cup besan or gram flour

1 tsp ground turmeric

¼ tsp chili powder

½–1 tsp salt, to taste

1¾ cups plain yogurt

2 tbsp ghee, vegetable oil, or peanut oil

scant 3 cups water

TO GARNISH

½ tbsp ghee, vegetable oil, or peanut oil

¾ tsp cumin seeds

½ tsp black mustard seeds

½ tsp fenugreek seeds

4–6 fresh red chilies, depending on how
    many people you are serving

18 HALDI DAHI KA SHORBA
turmeric yogurt soup

Mix the besan flour, turmeric, chili powder, and ½ teaspoon of salt together in a large bowl. Use a whisk or fork and beat in the yogurt until no lumps remain.

Melt the ghee in a wok or heavy-bottomed pan over medium-high heat. Mix in the yogurt mixture and then the water, whisking constantly. Bring to a boil, then reduce the heat to very low and simmer, still whisking frequently, for 8 minutes, or until the soup thickens slightly and doesn't have a "raw" taste any longer. Taste and stir in extra salt, if necessary.

In a separate small pan, melt the ghee for the garnish. Add the cumin, mustard, and fenugreek seeds, and stir around until the seeds start to jump and crackle. Add the chilies, remove the pan from the heat, and stir for about 30 seconds, or until the chilies blister (if the chilies are fresh, they might burst and "jump," so stand well back).

Ladle the soup into bowls and spoon the cooked spices over, including a little of the light brown ghee to serve.

COOK'S TIP
One technique for flavoring dal is to pour hot oil with cooked spices and leaves over the dish just before serving. This is called a tarka, or tempering, and is believed to bring the dish alive. If you don't want to temper the spices as detailed in the third paragraph, spoon a glob of coriander chutney into each portion instead.

SERVES 4–6

3 dried Chinese mushrooms, soaked in
warm water for 20 minutes

4 oz/115 g pork loin

2 oz/55 g fresh or canned bamboo
shoots, rinsed (if using fresh shoots,
boil in water first for 30 minutes)

8 oz/225 g firm bean curd
(drained weight)

3½ cups chicken bouillon

1 tbsp Shaoxing rice wine

1 tbsp light soy sauce

1½ tbsp white rice vinegar

1 tsp white pepper

1 tsp salt

1 egg, lightly beaten

SYUN LAAT TONG
hot-and-sour soup

Squeeze out any excess water from the mushrooms, then thinly slice, discarding any tough stems. Thinly slice the pork, bamboo shoots, and bean curd, all to a similar size.

Bring the bouillon to a boil in a large pan. Add the pork and boil over high heat for 2 minutes. Add the mushrooms and bamboo shoots and boil for another 2 minutes. Next, add the Shaoxing, light soy sauce, rice vinegar, pepper, and salt. Bring back to a boil and simmer, covered, for 5 minutes. Add the bean curd and boil, uncovered, for 2 minutes.

To serve, rapidly stir in the egg until it has formed fine shreds. Serve immediately.

COOK'S TIP
The heat in this soup comes from the liberal use of white pepper.

SERVES 4

4¼ cups beef bouillon

⅔ cup vegetable oil or peanut oil

3 oz/85 g rice vermicelli noodles

2 shallots, thinly sliced

2 garlic cloves, crushed

1-inch/2.5-cm piece fresh gingerroot,
 thinly sliced

8-oz/225-g piece tenderloin steak,
 cut into thin strips

2 tbsp Thai green curry paste

2 tbsp Thai soy sauce

1 tbsp Thai fish sauce

fresh cilantro, chopped, to garnish

GUAY TIAW TOM YAM NUEA
spicy beef and noodle soup

Pour the bouillon into a large pan and bring to a boil. Meanwhile, heat the oil in a wok or large skillet. Add a third of the noodles and cook for 10–20 seconds, or until they have puffed up. Lift out with tongs, drain on paper towels, and set aside. Discard all but 2 tablespoons of the oil.

Add the shallots, garlic, and gingerroot to the wok or skillet and stir-fry for 1 minute. Add the steak and curry paste and stir-fry for another 3–4 minutes, or until tender.

Add the beef mixture, the uncooked noodles, and the soy sauce and fish sauce to the pan of bouillon, and simmer for 2–3 minutes, or until the noodles have swelled. Serve hot, garnished with the chopped cilantro and the reserved crispy noodles.

SERVES 6–8

30 square won ton wrappers

1 egg white, lightly beaten

WON TON FILLING

6 oz/175 g ground pork, not too lean

8 oz/225 g raw shrimp, peeled, deveined,
    and chopped

½ tsp finely chopped fresh gingerroot

1 tbsp light soy sauce

1 tbsp Shaoxing rice wine

2 tsp finely chopped scallions

pinch of sugar

pinch of white pepper

dash of sesame oil

SOUP

scant 8½ cups chicken bouillon

2 tsp salt

½ tsp white pepper

2 tbsp finely chopped scallions

1 tbsp chopped fresh cilantro leaves,
    to serve

WUN TUN TONG
won ton soup

Mix together the filling ingredients in a bowl and stir well, until the texture is thick and pasty. Set aside for at least 20 minutes.

To make the won tons, place a teaspoon of the filling at the center of a wrapper. Brush the edges with a little egg white. Bring the opposite points toward each other and press the edges together, creating a flowerlike shape. Repeat with the remaining wrappers and filling.

To make the soup, bring the bouillon to a boil and add the salt and pepper. Boil the won tons in the bouillon for 5 minutes, or until the wrappers begin to wrinkle around the filling.

To serve, put the scallions in individual bowls, spoon in the won tons and soup, and top with the cilantro.

COOK'S TIP
Use the best chicken bouillon you have for this dish. Don't use a bouillon cube, because the broth needs almost to stand alone as a soup.

SERVES 4

3 large tomatoes

2 tbsp vegetable oil or peanut oil

4 shallots, finely chopped

2 garlic cloves, chopped

2 tsp ground turmeric

2 lemongrass stalks, snapped into
   three pieces

2 fresh green chilies, seeded and sliced

3 cilantro roots, chopped

3½ cups fish bouillon

2 tsp jaggery or soft, light brown sugar

2 tbsp Thai fish sauce

12 raw jumbo shrimp, peeled with tails
   left intact

8 oz/225 g live mussels, scrubbed
   and debearded

8 oz/225 g white fish fillet, skinned and
   cut into large cubes

8 oz/225 g squid, cut into rings

juice of 1 lime

few sprigs of fresh Thai basil

TOM JOOD TA-LA SAI BAI HU LA PA
seafood and basil soup

Bring a pot of water to a boil. Cut a small cross in the top of each tomato, then drop it in the boiling water for about 1 minute. Remove the tomatoes from the hot water and immediately plunge into ice-cold water. Skin the tomatoes, then cut them in half, scoop out the seeds, and very finely dice the flesh.

Heat the oil in a wok or large skillet and stir-fry the shallots, garlic, turmeric, lemongrass, chilies, and cilantro for 1–2 minutes to release the flavors.

Add the chopped tomatoes, bouillon, jaggery, and fish sauce, and simmer for 8–10 minutes.

Add the shrimp, mussels, white fish cubes, and squid rings to the wok or skillet, cover, and simmer for 3–5 minutes, or until the fish is cooked and the mussels have opened. Discard any mussels that remain closed. Stir in the lime juice and Thai basil sprigs, ladle into warmed bowls, and serve immediately.

MAKES 14

DOUGH

2¼ cups all-purpose flour

½ tsp salt

3 tbsp ghee or unsalted
   butter, melted, plus extra
   for greasing

½ tbsp lemon juice

about ½ cup cold water

fresh cilantro sprigs, to garnish

FILLING

4 tbsp ghee, vegetable oil, or
   peanut oil

1 onion, very finely chopped

2 garlic cloves, crushed

1 potato, very finely diced

2 carrots, very finely chopped

2 tsp mild, medium, or hot
   curry powder, to taste

1½ tsp ground coriander

1 tsp ground turmeric

1 fresh green chili, seeded and
   finely chopped

1 tsp salt

½ tsp black mustard seeds

1¼ cups water

scant 1 cup frozen peas

2 oz/55 g cauliflower florets,
   broken into the smallest
   florets possible

vegetable oil or peanut oil,
   for cooking

ALOO MATTAR SAMOSA
vegetarian samosas

To make the filling, melt the ghee in a large skillet over medium-high heat. Add the onion and garlic and cook for 5–8 minutes, until soft. Stir in the potato and carrots and cook, stirring occasionally, for 5 minutes. Stir in the curry powder, coriander, turmeric, chili, salt, and mustard seeds. Add the water and bring to a boil. Reduce the heat to very low and simmer, uncovered, for 15 minutes, stirring occasionally. Add the peas and cauliflower florets and simmer until the vegetables are tender and the liquid evaporates. Remove from the heat and set aside.

To make the dough, sift the flour and salt into a bowl. Make a well in the center, add the ghee and lemon juice, and work into the flour with your fingertips. Gradually add the water to form a soft dough. Tip the dough onto a counter and knead for 10 minutes, or until smooth. Shape into a ball, cover with a damp dish towel, and let rest for 15 minutes.

To shape the dough, divide into 7 equal pieces. Work with 1 piece at a time and keep the remaining pieces covered with a dish towel. Roll each piece into an 8-inch/20-cm circle on a greased counter, then cut in half to make 2 semicircles. Cut out 12 more semicircles.

Working with one semicircle at a time, wet the edges with water. Place 2 teaspoons of the filling on the dough, just off-center. Fold one side into the center, covering the filling. Fold the other side across, overlapping the first fold to form a cone. Wet the open edge with water and press to seal. Cover the finished samosas with a damp dish towel while you work on the rest.

Heat 1 inch/2.5 cm of oil in a heavy-bottomed pan, until it reaches 350–375°F/180–190°C, or a cube of bread browns in 30 seconds. Cook the samosas in batches for 2–3 minutes, turning once, until golden brown. Drain on paper towels. Serve warm, garnished with cilantro sprigs.

MAKES 18–20

6 dried Chinese mushrooms, soaked in warm water for 20 minutes

2 oz/55 g beanthread noodles, soaked in warm water for 20 minutes

2 tbsp vegetable oil or peanut oil, plus extra for deep-frying

1 tbsp finely chopped fresh gingerroot

⅔ cup julienned carrot

1 cup finely shredded cabbage

1 tbsp thinly sliced scallion

1 tbsp light soy sauce, plus extra to serve

3 oz/85 g soft bean curd (drained weight), cut into small cubes

½ tsp salt

pinch of white pepper

pinch of sugar

20 soft spring roll wrappers

1 egg white, lightly beaten

30 SOU CHOI CHEUN GYUN
vegetarian spring rolls

Squeeze any excess water from the mushrooms and finely chop, discarding any tough stems. Drain the beanthread noodles and coarsely chop.

In a preheated wok or deep pan, heat 2 tablespoons of the oil, toss in the ginger, and cook until fragrant. Add the mushrooms and stir for about 2 minutes. Add the carrot, cabbage, and scallion, and stir-fry for 1 minute. Add the beanthread noodles and light soy sauce and stir-fry for 1 minute. Add the bean curd and cook for another minute. Season with the salt, pepper, and sugar and mix well. Continue cooking for 1–2 minutes, or until the carrot is soft. Remove from the heat and let the mixture cool.

Place about a tablespoon of the mixture toward the bottom of a wrapper. Roll once to secure the filling, then fold in the sides to create a 4-inch/10-cm piece and continue to roll up. Seal with egg white.

Heat enough oil for deep-frying in a wok, deep-fat fryer, or large, heavy-bottomed pan, until it reaches 350–375°F/180–190°C, or until a cube of bread browns in 30 seconds. Without overcrowding the pan, cook the rolls for 5 minutes, or until golden brown and crispy. Serve with a good soy sauce for dipping.

VARIATION
They are less authentic, but delicious small-size rolls can be made with rice-paper wrappers, brushed with hot water to soften them. These are also easier to handle than wheat wrappers.

SERVES 4–6

14 oz/400 g new potatoes, scrubbed

1 tsp coriander seeds

1 tsp fennel seeds

1¾ cups plain yogurt

1 fresh green chili, seeded and
  finely chopped

salt and pepper

fresh mint, chopped, to garnish

4–8 pappadams, warmed, to serve

ALOO KA RAITA
raita potatoes

Boil the potatoes in salted water for 10–12 minutes, or until tender when pierced with a fork. Drain and rinse with cold water to cool, then shake dry. When cool enough to handle, finely chop the potatoes, with or without peeling them.

Meanwhile, dry-cook the coriander and fennel seeds in a hot skillet over high heat, stirring them around constantly, until you can smell the aromas. Immediately tip the spices out of the pan so they do not burn.

Put the spices in a spice grinder or use a pestle and mortar to grind to a fine powder. Beat the yogurt in a bowl until it is smooth, then stir in the ground spices and chili, and salt and pepper to taste. Add the potato chunks and stir together without breaking up the potatoes. Cover the bowl with plastic wrap and chill for at least 30 minutes.

When ready to serve, give the potatoes and yogurt a quick stir, then add lots of chopped fresh mint. Serve with warm pappadams.

COOK'S TIP
To warm pappadams, heat about ½ inch/1 cm vegetable oil or peanut oil in a wok or large skillet. Add each pappadam and cook for a few seconds, until it expands, turns pale golden-brown, and small bubbles appear all over the surface. Use tongs to remove from the pan and drain on crumpled paper towels. Alternatively, preheat the broiler to its highest setting. Brush each pappadam with a little vegetable oil or peanut oil and broil for a few seconds on each side.

SERVES 4

vegetable oil or peanut oil,
   for deep-frying
14 oz/400 g cauliflower florets
chutney, to serve

BATTER

1¼ cups besan or gram flour
2 tsp ground coriander

1 tsp garam masala
1 tsp salt
½ tsp ground turmeric
pinch of chili powder
1 tbsp ghee, melted, or 1 tbsp vegetable
   oil or peanut oil
1 tsp lemon juice
⅔ cup cold water
2 tsp nigella seeds

GOBHI KA PAKORA
golden cauliflower pakoras

To make the batter, place the besan flour, coriander, garam masala, salt, turmeric, and chili powder in a large bowl and stir together well. Make a well in the center, add the ghee and lemon juice with 2 tablespoons of the water, and stir together to make a thick batter.

Slowly beat in enough of the remaining water with an electric hand-held mixer or a whisk to make a smooth batter about the same thickness as heavy cream. Stir in the nigella seeds. Cover the bowl with plastic wrap and set aside to stand for at least 30 minutes.

Heat enough oil for deep-frying in a wok, deep-fat fryer, or large, heavy-bottomed pan, until it reaches 350–375°F/180–190°C, or until a cube of bread browns in 30 seconds. Dip one cauliflower floret at a time into the batter and let any excess batter fall back into the bowl, then drop it into the hot oil. Add a few more dipped florets, without overcrowding the pan, and cook for 3 minutes, or until golden brown and crisp.

Use a slotted spoon to remove the fritters from the oil and drain well on crumpled paper towels. Continue cooking until all the cauliflower florets and batter have been used. Serve the hot fritters with a chutney for dipping.

MAKES 12

1¼ cups besan or gram flour

1 tsp salt

1 tsp ground cumin

1 tsp ground turmeric

1 tsp baking soda

½ tsp chili powder

2 tsp lemon juice

2 tbsp vegetable oil or peanut oil, plus
   extra for deep-frying

2–8 tbsp water

2 onions, thinly sliced

2 tsp coriander seeds, lightly crushed

lemon wedges, to serve

PYAAZ PAKORA
onion bhajias

Sift the besan flour, salt, cumin, turmeric, baking soda, and chili powder into a large bowl. Add the lemon juice and 2 tablespoons of the oil, then very gradually stir in just enough water until a batter similar to light cream forms. Mix in the onions and coriander seeds.

Heat enough oil for deep-frying in a wok, deep-fat fryer, or large, heavy-bottomed pan, until it reaches 350–375°F/180–190°C, or until a cube of bread browns in 30 seconds. Without overcrowding the pan, drop in spoonfuls of the onion mixture and cook for 2 minutes, then use tongs to flip the bhajias over and continue cooking for another 2 minutes, or until golden brown.

Immediately remove the bhajias from the oil and drain well on crumpled paper towels. Keep the bhajias warm while you continue cooking the remaining batter. Serve hot with lemon wedges for squeezing over.

COOK'S TIP

As with all deep-fried food, the fine line between light crispiness and greasiness depends on keeping the oil at the correct temperature while the bhajias are cooking. If it is too low, the bhajias will be greasy; too hot, and the coating will burn while the onions remain raw. This is why you should cook the bhajias in batches and let the oil return to the correct temperature between batches. If you do lots of deep-fat frying, it is worth investing in a thermometer.

SERVES 4

2 tbsp vegetable oil or peanut oil

1 tbsp sesame oil

juice of ½ lime

2 skinned, boned chicken breast
    portions, cut into small cubes

TO SERVE

slices of cucumber

boiled rice

DIP

2 tbsp vegetable oil or peanut oil

1 small onion, finely chopped

1 small fresh green chili, seeded
    and chopped

1 garlic clove, finely chopped

½ cup crunchy peanut butter

6–8 tbsp water

juice of ½ lime

SATAY GAI
chicken satay

Combine both the oils and the lime juice in a nonmetallic dish. Add the chicken cubes, cover with plastic wrap, and chill for 1 hour.

To make the dip, heat the oil in a skillet and cook the onion, chili, and garlic over low heat, stirring occasionally, for 5 minutes, or until just softened. Add the peanut butter, 6 tablespoons of water, and the lime juice, and simmer gently, stirring constantly, until the peanut butter has softened enough to make a dip—you may need to add extra water to make a thinner consistency.

Meanwhile, drain the chicken cubes and thread them onto 8–12 wooden skewers. Put under a hot broiler or on a barbecue grill, turning frequently, for 10 minutes, or until cooked and browned. Serve hot with the warm dip, the slices of cucumber, and the boiled rice.

COOK'S TIP
Soak wooden skewers in cold water for 45 minutes before threading the meat to help stop them from burning during cooking.

SERVES 3–4

9 oz/250 g chicken wings, thawed
   if frozen

scant 1 cup water

1 tbsp sliced scallion

1-inch/2.5-cm piece fresh gingerroot, cut
   into 4 slices

2 tbsp light soy sauce

½ tsp dark soy sauce

1 star anise

1 tsp sugar

SI YAU GAI YIK
soy chicken wings

Wash the chicken wings and dry with paper towels. In a small pan, bring the water to a boil, then add the chicken, scallion, and gingerroot, and bring back to a boil.

Add the remaining ingredients, cover, and simmer for 30 minutes.

Remove the chicken wings from any remaining liquid and serve hot.

SERVES 4

2 tbsp vegetable oil or peanut oil

2 red onions, thinly sliced

2 garlic cloves, chopped

1-inch/2.5-cm piece gingerroot, cut
into batons

8 oz/225 g beef tenderloin, thinly sliced
into strips

1 green bell pepper, seeded and sliced

2 cups canned bamboo shoots

2 cups bean sprouts

2 tbsp Thai magic paste

1 tbsp Thai red curry paste

2 tbsp chopped fresh cilantro

few sprigs of Thai basil

boiled rice, to serve

42

PAHD NUEA
beef stir-fry

Heat the oil in a wok or large skillet and stir-fry the onions, garlic, and gingerroot for 1 minute. Add the beef strips and cook over high heat, until browned all over. Add the vegetables and the two pastes and cook for 2–3 minutes, or until blended and cooked.

Stir in the cilantro and basil and serve immediately with boiled rice.

MAKES 20

4 oz/115 g firm bean curd
  (drained weight)

3 tbsp vegetable oil or peanut oil

1 tsp finely chopped garlic

2 oz/55 g lean pork, shredded

4 oz/115 g raw shrimp, peeled
  and deveined

½ small carrot, cut into batons

2 oz/55 g fresh or canned bamboo
  shoots, rinsed and shredded (if using
  fresh shoots, boil in water first for
  30 minutes)

4 oz/115 g cabbage, very finely sliced

2 oz/55 g snow peas, julienned

1-egg omelet, shredded

1 tsp salt

1 tsp light soy sauce

1 tsp Shaoxing rice wine

pinch of white pepper

20 soft spring roll wrappers

chili bean sauce, to serve

CHUNG SIK YUT NAAM CHEUN GYUN

soft-wrapped pork and shrimp rolls

Slice the bean curd into thin slices horizontally and cook in 1 tablespoon of the oil until it turns golden brown. Remove from the pan, cut into thin strips, and set aside.

In a preheated wok or deep pan, heat the remaining oil and stir-fry the garlic until fragrant. Add the pork and stir for about 1 minute, then add the shrimp and stir for another minute. One by one, stirring well after each, add the carrot, bamboo shoots, cabbage, snow peas, bean curd, and, finally, the omelet pieces. Season with the salt, light soy sauce, Shaoxing rice wine, and pepper. Stir for another minute, then turn into a serving dish.

To assemble each roll, smear a wrapper with a little chili bean sauce and place a heaping teaspoon of the filling toward the bottom of the circle. Roll up the bottom edge to secure the filling, turn in the sides, and continue to roll up gently.

COOK'S TIP
Chill the firm bean curd in advance to make it easier to handle.

SERVES 4–6

2 tomatoes

¼ tsp ground coriander

¼ tsp ground cumin

¼ tsp garam masala

1 onion, very finely chopped

1¾ cups seeded and finely
    diced cucumber

9 oz/250 g small cooked, peeled shrimp,
    thawed if frozen

3 tbsp chopped fresh cilantro

salt

TO SERVE

6–8 Pooris

lemon wedges

MASALA JHINGA AUR KAKDI

spicy shrimp with cucumber

Bring a pan of water to a boil. Cut a small cross in the top of each tomato, then drop it in the boiling water for about 1 minute. Remove the tomatoes from the hot water and immediately plunge into ice-cold water. Skin the tomatoes, then cut them in half, scoop out the seeds, and very finely dice the flesh.

Put the coriander, cumin, and garam masala in a dry skillet over medium-high heat and stir for 15 seconds. Add the onion and continue stirring constantly for 2 minutes—the mixture will be very dry.

Add the tomatoes and cucumber to the pan and stir for 2 minutes. Add the shrimp and stir for another 2 minutes just to warm them through. Stir in the cilantro and salt to taste.

Serve hot or at room temperature with the pooris, and lemon wedges for squeezing over.

VARIATION

For a colorful, refreshing version, replace the cucumber with finely diced mango and serve chilled.

SERVES 4

6 oz/175 g whitebait

1 tbsp vegetable oil or peanut oil

1 large fresh green chili

2 drops of sesame oil

1 tbsp light soy sauce

pinch of salt

pinch of sugar

1 garlic clove, finely chopped

LAAT MEI BAAT FAAN YU
whitebait with green chili

In a large pan of boiling water, cook the fish for 30 seconds–2 minutes, or until the flesh is turning soft but not breaking up. Drain, set aside, and cool.

To prepare the sauce, first heat the oil in a small pan and, when smoking, cook the chili until the skin blisters. Remove the skin and finely chop the chili. When cool, mix in a bowl with all the other ingredients.

Pour the sauce over the fish and serve immediately.

COOK'S TIP
Whitebait have a tendency to stick together and break easily once cooked, so treat with care.

SERVES 4

1 lb/450 g white fish fillets, skinned and cut into cubes

1 egg white

2 kaffir lime leaves, coarsely torn

1 tbsp Thai green curry paste

2 oz/55 g green beans, finely chopped

1 fresh red chili, seeded and finely chopped

bunch of fresh cilantro, chopped

vegetable oil or peanut oil, for cooking

1 fresh green chili, seeded and sliced, to serve

DIPPING SAUCE

generous ½ cup superfine sugar

1½ tbsp water

generous 3 tbsp white wine vinegar

1 small carrot, cut into thin batons

2-inch/5-cm piece cucumber, peeled, seeded, and cut into thin batons

THOT MAN PLA
fish cakes

Put the fish into a food processor with the egg white, lime leaves, and curry paste, and process until smooth. Scrape the mixture into a bowl and stir in the green beans, red chili, and cilantro.

With dampened hands, shape the mixture into small patties, about 2 inches/5 cm across. Place them on a large plate in a single layer and chill for 30 minutes.

Meanwhile, make the Dipping Sauce. Put the sugar in a pan with the water and vinegar and heat gently, stirring, until the sugar has dissolved. Add the carrot and cucumber, then remove from the heat and let cool.

Heat the oil in a skillet and cook the fish cakes, in batches, until golden-brown on both sides. Drain on paper towels and keep warm while you cook the remaining batches. Serve the fish cakes immediately with warm or cold dipping sauce, topped with chili slices.

MAKES 20

12 oz/350 g canned white
   crabmeat, drained
1 fresh red chili, seeded and chopped
4 scallions, thinly sliced
1 tbsp Thai red curry paste
juice of ½ lime
½ tsp salt
20 won ton wrappers
vegetable oil or peanut oil,
   for deep-frying

DIPPING SAUCE

4½ tbsp superfine sugar
2 tbsp water
2 tbsp rice wine vinegar
3 pieces preserved ginger, sliced
1 tbsp ginger syrup

PUE HAO
crab parcels

Put the crabmeat into a bowl and add the chili, scallions, and curry paste. Stir together with the lime juice and salt.

Put the wrappers in a pile and put 1 portion of the crabmeat in the middle of the top wrapper. Brush the edges with a little water and roll up the edges to make a small, cigar-shaped packet. Continue to make packets until you run out of crabmeat.

Heat the oil in a wok or large skillet and cook the packets, a few at a time, until golden brown. Drain on paper towels.

Put all the ingredients for the Dipping Sauce in a small pan and heat gently until the sugar has dissolved. Serve warm with the crab packets.

Meat and Poultry

SERVES 4–6

14 oz/400 g canned chopped tomatoes

1¼ cups heavy cream

8 pieces cooked tandoori chicken

sprigs of fresh cilantro, to garnish

TIKKA MASALA

2 tbsp ghee, vegetable oil, or peanut oil

1 large garlic clove, finely chopped

1 fresh red chili, seeded and chopped

2 tsp ground cumin

2 tsp ground paprika

½ tsp salt

black pepper

MURGH TIKKA MAKHANI
chicken tikka masala

To make the Tikka Masala, melt the ghee or heat the oil in a large skillet with a lid over medium heat. Add the garlic and chili and stir-fry for 1 minute. Stir in the cumin, paprika, and salt, and pepper to taste, and continue stirring for about 30 seconds.

Stir the tomatoes, with their juices, and the cream into the pan. Reduce the heat to low and let the sauce simmer for about 10 minutes, stirring frequently, until it reduces and thickens.

Meanwhile, remove all the bones and any skin from the tandoori chicken pieces, then cut the meat into bite-size pieces.

Adjust the seasoning of the sauce, if necessary. Add the chicken pieces to the pan, cover, and let simmer for 3–5 minutes, or until the chicken is heated through. Garnish with the cilantro to serve.

COOK'S TIP
This Asian dish reputedly started life in British restaurants as a way to use up leftover cooked tandoori chicken, though now it is prepared in Asian restaurants. Use cooked tandoori chicken pieces from a supermarket or an Asian take-out, or any leftovers if you've cooked your own.

SERVES 4

12 oz/350 g boneless, skinless
  chicken meat
few drops of sesame oil
2 tbsp sesame paste
1 tbsp light soy sauce
1 tbsp chicken bouillon
½ tsp salt
pinch of sugar

TO SERVE

8 tbsp shredded lettuce leaves
1 tbsp sesame seeds, roasted

PANG PANG GAI
bang bang chicken

Place the chicken in a pan of cold water, bring to a boil, and simmer for 8–10 minutes. Drain, let cool a little, then cut or tear the chicken into bite-size pieces.

Mix together the sesame oil, sesame paste, light soy sauce, chicken bouillon, salt, and sugar, and whisk until the sauce is thick and smooth. Toss in the chicken.

To serve, put the shredded lettuce on a large plate and spoon the chicken and sauce on top. Sprinkle with the sesame seeds and serve at room temperature.

SERVES 4–6

4 tbsp ghee, vegetable oil, or peanut oil

8 skinless, boneless chicken
thighs, sliced

1 large onion, chopped

2 tbsp Garlic and Ginger Paste

2 green bell peppers, cored, seeded,
and chopped

1 large fresh green chili, seeded
and finely chopped

1 tsp ground cumin

1 tsp ground coriander

¼–½ tsp chili powder

½ tsp ground turmeric

¼ tsp salt

14 oz/400 g canned chopped tomatoes

½ cup water

fresh cilantro, chopped, to garnish

chicken jalfrezi

Melt half the ghee in a wok or large skillet over medium-high heat. Add the chicken slices and stir for 5 minutes, or until browned but not necessarily cooked through, then remove from the pan with a slotted spoon and set aside.

Melt the remaining ghee in the pan. Add the onion and cook, stirring frequently, for 5–8 minutes, or until golden brown. Stir in the garlic and ginger paste and continue cooking for 2 minutes, stirring frequently.

Add the bell peppers to the pan and stir around for 2 minutes.

Stir in the chili, cumin, coriander, chili powder, turmeric, and salt. Add the tomatoes with their juice, and the water, and bring to a boil.

Reduce the heat to low, add the chicken, and let it simmer, uncovered, for 10 minutes, stirring frequently, until the bell peppers are tender, the chicken is cooked through, and the juices run clear if you pierce a few pieces with the tip of a knife. Sprinkle with the chopped cilantro and serve immediately.

VARIATION
To make this into a more satisfying meal that doesn't need any accompanying rice, add 14 oz/400 g chopped new potatoes with the tomatoes and water. Bring to a boil, then lower the heat, and simmer for 5 minutes before you add the chicken.

SERVES 4

3 skinned, boned chicken breast
  portions, cut into cubes
juice of 1 lime
1-inch/2.5-cm piece gingerroot,
  peeled and chopped
1 fresh red chili, seeded and sliced
2 tbsp vegetable oil or peanut oil
1 onion, sliced
2 garlic cloves, chopped
1 eggplant, cut into chunks

2 zucchini, thickly sliced
1 red bell pepper, cored, seeded,
  and cut into squares
2 tbsp Thai red curry paste
2 tbsp Thai soy sauce
1 tsp jaggery or soft, light
  brown sugar
few sprigs of fresh cilantro, to garnish
boiled rice with chopped fresh cilantro,
  to serve

62 KEBAB GAI KHING
gingered chicken kabobs

Put the chicken cubes in a shallow dish. Mix the lime, gingerroot, and chili together and pour over the chicken pieces. Stir gently to coat. Cover and chill for at least 3 hours to marinate.

Soak wooden skewers in cold water for 45 minutes before threading the meat to help stop them from burning during cooking.

Thread the chicken pieces onto the skewers and cook under a hot broiler for 3–4 minutes, turning often, until cooked through.

Meanwhile, heat the oil in a wok or large skillet and cook the onion and garlic for 1–2 minutes, or until softened but not browned. Add the eggplant, zucchini, and bell pepper, and cook for 3–4 minutes, or until cooked but still firm. Add the curry paste, soy sauce, and jaggery and cook for 1 minute.

Serve hot with boiled rice stirred through with chopped cilantro and use some sprigs as a garnish.

SERVES 4

generous 1 cup jasmine rice

3 skinned, boned chicken breasts, cut
 into cubes

1¾ cups canned coconut milk

3–4 tbsp coconut cream

2–3 cilantro roots, chopped

thinly pared zest of 1 lemon

1 fresh green chili, seeded and chopped

3 fresh Thai basil leaves

1 tbsp Thai fish sauce

1 tbsp vegetable or peanut oil

3 eggs, beaten

TO GARNISH

long fresh chives

few sprigs of fresh cilantro

64 KHAO PHAT GAI SAI KHAI
egg-fried rice
with chicken

Cook the rice in boiling water for 12–15 minutes, drain well, then cool, cover with plastic wrap immediately, and chill overnight.

Put the chicken into a pan and cover with the coconut milk. Add the coconut cream, cilantro roots, lemon zest, and chili, and bring to a boil. Simmer for 8–10 minutes, or until the chicken is tender. Remove from the heat. Stir in the basil and fish sauce.

Meanwhile, heat the oil in a wok and stir-fry the rice for 2–3 minutes. Pour in the eggs and stir until they have cooked and mixed with the rice. Line 4 small pudding molds or ramekins with plastic wrap and pack with the rice. Turn out carefully onto serving plates and remove the plastic wrap. Garnish with long chives and sprigs of cilantro. Serve with the chicken.

SERVES 6–10

1 duckling, weighing 4 lb 8 oz/2 kg

6⅓ cups boiling water

1 tbsp honey

1 tbsp Shaoxing rice wine

1 tsp white rice vinegar

1 cucumber, peeled, seeded,
   and julienned

10 scallions, white parts only, shredded

30 Peking duck crêpes

plum sauce or Peking sauce, to serve

BAK GING TIN NGAAP
peking duck

To prepare the duck, massage the skin to separate it from the meat.

Pour the boiling water into a large pan, add the honey, Shaoxing, and vinegar, and lower in the duck. Baste for about 1 minute. Remove the duck and hang it to dry for a few hours or overnight.

Preheat the oven to 400°F/200°C. Place the duck on a rack above a roasting pan and roast for at least 1 hour, or until the skin is very crispy and the duck cooked through.

Bring the duck to the table, together with the cucumber, scallions, and crêpes, and carve off the skin first. On a crêpe, arrange a little skin with some cucumber and scallion pieces. Top with a little plum sauce or Peking sauce, or both. Roll up and eat. Repeat the process with the lean meat.

SERVES 4

4 tomatoes

1 tbsp vegetable oil or peanut oil

2 duck breasts, skin on

1 onion, sliced

2 garlic cloves, chopped

1 red bell pepper, cored, seeded,
   and sliced

1 green bell pepper, cored, seeded,
   and sliced

1 yellow bell pepper, cored, seeded,
   and sliced

⅔ cup bouillon

3 tbsp Thai soy sauce

boiled noodles, to serve

PED KUB PHRIK THAI
duck with mixed bell peppers

Bring a pan of water to a boil. Cut a small cross in the top of each tomato, then drop it in the boiling water for about 1 minute. Remove the tomatoes from the hot water and immediately plunge into ice-cold water. Skin the tomatoes, then cut them in half, scoop out the seeds, and very finely dice the flesh.

Heat the oil in a wok and cook the duck breasts over high heat, until crisp and brown. Turn over and cook until tender all through. Lift out and keep warm.

Pour off any excess fat, add the onion and garlic, and stir-fry for 2–3 minutes, or until softened and lightly browned.

Add the bell peppers and stir-fry for 2–3 minutes, or until tender. Add the tomatoes, bouillon, and soy sauce and simmer for 1–2 minutes. Transfer to a serving plate. Slice the duck thickly and arrange on top, spooning any sauce over it. Serve immediately with boiled noodles.

SERVES 4

10 oz/280 g tenderloin steak, cut
    into strips

8 oz/225 g dried egg noodles

2 tbsp vegetable oil or peanut oil

1 onion, thinly sliced

1 green bell pepper, cored, seeded,
    and thinly sliced

2½ cups bean sprouts, trimmed

1 tsp salt

pinch of sugar

2 tsp Shaoxing rice wine

2 tbsp light soy sauce

1 tbsp dark soy sauce

1 tbsp finely shredded scallion

MARINADE

1 tsp light soy sauce

dash of sesame oil

½ tsp Shaoxing rice wine

pinch of white pepper

NGAU YUK CHAAU MIN
beef chow mein

Combine all the marinade ingredients in a bowl, add the beef, and marinate for at least 20 minutes.

Cook the noodles according to the instructions on the package. When cooked, rinse under cold water and set aside.

In a preheated wok or deep skillet, heat the oil and stir-fry the beef for 1 minute, or until the meat has changed color, then add the onion and cook for 1 minute, followed by the bell pepper and bean sprouts. When the water has evaporated from the vegetables, add the salt, sugar, Shaoxing, and soy sauces. Stir in the noodles and toss for 1 minute. Finally, stir in the scallion and serve.

VARIATION
To make this dish with crispy noodles, flash-fry the noodles after cooking them.

SERVES 4–6

1–2 dried red chilies

2 tsp ground coriander

2 tsp ground turmeric

1 tsp black mustard seeds

½ tsp ground ginger

¼ tsp ground pepper

1¼ cups coconut cream

4 tbsp ghee, vegetable oil, or peanut oil

2 onions, chopped

3 large garlic cloves, chopped

1 lb 9 oz/700 g lean stewing steak, such as chuck, trimmed and cut into 2-inch/5-cm cubes

generous 1 cup beef bouillon, plus a little extra if necessary

lemon juice

salt

few sprigs of fresh cilantro, to garnish

MADRASI GOSHT
beef madras

Depending on how hot you want this dish to be, chop the chilies with or without any seeds. The more seeds you include, the hotter the dish will be. Put the chopped chilies and any seeds in a small bowl with the coriander, turmeric, mustard seeds, ginger, and pepper and stir in a little of the coconut cream to make a thin paste.

Melt the ghee in a flameproof casserole or large skillet with a tight-fitting lid over medium-high heat. Add the onions and garlic and cook for 5–8 minutes, stirring often, until the onion is golden brown. Add the spice paste and stir for 2 minutes, or until you can smell the aromas.

Add the meat and bouillon and bring to a boil. Reduce the heat to its lowest level, cover tightly, and simmer for 1½ hours, or until the beef is tender when you pierce it with a fork. Check occasionally that the meat isn't catching on the bottom of the pan, and stir in a little extra water or bouillon, if necessary.

Uncover the pan and stir in the remaining coconut cream with the lemon juice and salt to taste. Bring to a boil, stirring, then lower the heat again and simmer, still uncovered, until the sauce reduces slightly. Serve hot, garnished with fresh cilantro.

VARIATION
The dish takes on a different character, but is equally flavorsome, if you omit the chilies altogether and garnish the dish with toasted coconut flakes just before serving.

SERVES 4

1 lb/450 g rib eye or sirloin steak,
  thinly sliced

1 head broccoli, cut into small florets

2 tbsp vegetable oil or peanut oil

1 onion, thinly sliced

2 celery stalks, thinly sliced diagonally

3 cups snow peas, sliced in half lengthwise

2 oz/55 g fresh or canned bamboo shoots,
  rinsed and julienned (if using fresh
  shoots, boil in water first for 30 minutes)

8 water chestnuts, finely sliced

3¼ cups thinly sliced mushrooms

1 tbsp oyster sauce

1 tsp salt

boiled rice, to serve

MARINADE

1 tbsp Shaoxing rice wine

pinch of white pepper

pinch of salt

1 tbsp light soy sauce

½ tsp sesame oil

JAAP SEUI NGAU YUK
beef chop suey

Combine the marinade ingredients in a bowl with the beef and marinate for at least
20 minutes. Blanch the broccoli in a large pan of boiling water for 30 seconds. Drain and
set aside.

In a preheated wok or deep pan, heat 1 tablespoon of the oil and stir-fry the beef until the color
has changed. Remove the beef and set aside.

Clean your wok or pan, heat the remaining oil, and stir-fry the onion for 1 minute. Add the
celery and broccoli and cook for 2 minutes. Add the snow peas, bamboo shoots, chestnuts, and
mushrooms and cook for 1 minute. Add the beef, season with the oyster sauce and salt, and
serve with boiled rice.

COOK'S TIP
Most restaurants would use cornstarch to thicken the sauce. This is a fresh-tasting version,
and any water from the vegetables evaporates in the wok.

SERVES 4

1 tbsp vegetable oil or peanut oil

1 large dried chili, seeded and snipped
   into 3 pieces

½ tsp Sichuan peppers

3½ oz/100 g ground beef

2 tsp light soy sauce

10½ oz/300 g fine white noodles

1 tbsp roasted peanuts, chopped

SAUCE

1 tbsp preserved vegetables

½ tsp Sichuan peppers, lightly roasted
   and crushed

scant ⅓ cup chicken bouillon

1 tsp black Chinese vinegar

1 tsp chili oil

1 tsp dark soy sauce

1 tbsp light soy sauce

1 tbsp sesame paste

few drops of sesame oil

2 scallions, finely chopped

DAAM DAAM MIN
dan dan mian

Heat the oil in a preheated wok or deep pan, toss in the chili and peppers, then add the meat and stir rapidly. When the meat has changed color, add the light soy sauce and continue to cook until the meat is well browned.

Carefully mix the sauce ingredients together and pour into 4 noodle bowls.

Cook the noodles according to the instructions on the package. When cooked, drain and divide among the bowls.

Top with the meat mixture, sprinkle with the roasted peanuts, and serve immediately. Mix well before eating.

COOK'S TIP
This is quite a dry noodle dish. Add more chicken bouillon if you prefer a greater quantity of sauce.

SERVES 4

1 lb/450 g bean curd (drained weight)

2 tbsp vegetable oil or peanut oil

1 tsp Sichuan peppers

3½ oz/100 g ground beef

2 tbsp chili bean sauce

1 tsp fermented black beans, rinsed
   and lightly mashed

scant ½ cup hot chicken bouillon

pinch of sugar

1 tsp light soy sauce

pinch of salt

2 tbsp thinly sliced scallion,
   cut on the diagonal

MA PO DAU FU

beef and bean curd stir-fry

Cut the bean curd into ¾-inch/2-cm cubes and arrange in a large pan. Pour over enough boiling water to cover and let rest.

In a preheated wok or deep pan, heat the oil until almost smoking. Throw in the Sichuan pepper and stir until fragrant. Add the beef and stir-fry until brown and crispy.

Lower the heat, add the chili bean sauce and black beans, and stir for 30 seconds, or until the oil is a rich red color.

Pour in the hot chicken bouillon and gently add the drained bean curd. Season with the sugar, light soy sauce, and salt. Simmer for about 5 minutes.

Finally, toss in the scallion. Transfer into 1 large or 4 individual bowls and serve.

SERVES 4

1 lb/450 g spareribs, cut into bite-size
   pieces (you or your butcher can cut
   ribs into pieces with a cleaver)
vegetable oil or peanut oil, for
   deep-frying

MARINADE

2 tsp light soy sauce
½ tsp salt
pinch of white pepper

SAUCE

3 tbsp white rice vinegar
2 tbsp sugar
1 tbsp light soy sauce
1 tbsp tomato ketchup
1½ tbsp vegetable oil or peanut oil
1 green bell pepper, cored, seeded,
   and coarsely chopped
1 small onion, coarsely chopped
1 small carrot, thinly sliced
½ tsp finely chopped garlic
½ tsp finely chopped gingerroot
3½ oz/100 g pineapple chunks

TONG CHOU PAAI GWAT
spareribs in a sweet-and-sour sauce

Combine the marinade ingredients in a bowl with the spareribs and marinate for at least
20 minutes.

Heat enough oil for deep-frying in a wok, deep-fat fryer, or large, heavy-bottomed pan until it
reaches 350–375°F/180–190°C, or until a cube of bread browns in 30 seconds. Deep-fry the
spareribs for 8 minutes. Drain and set aside.

To prepare the sauce, first mix together the vinegar, sugar, light soy sauce, and ketchup.
Set aside.

In a preheated wok or deep pan, heat 1 tablespoon of the oil and stir-fry the bell pepper, onion,
and carrot for 2 minutes. Remove and set aside.

Clean your wok or pan and heat the remaining oil and stir-fry the garlic and gingerroot until
fragrant. Add the vinegar mixture. Bring back to a boil and add the pineapple cubes. Finally,
add the spareribs and the bell pepper, onion, and carrot. Stir until warmed through and serve.

COOK'S TIP
This dish is usually made with canned pineapple chunks, but fresh pineapple provides a more
interesting, if slightly less sweet, flavor.

SERVES 4

½ cup vegetable oil or peanut oil

4 oz/115 g rice vermicelli noodles

4 thick side pork slices

1 red onion, sliced

2 garlic cloves, chopped

1-inch/2.5-cm piece fresh gingerroot,
   thinly sliced

1 large fresh red chili, seeded
   and chopped

1 cup baby corn, halved lengthwise

1 red bell pepper, cored, seeded,
   and sliced

6 oz/175 g broccoli, cut into florets

⅔ cup black bean sauce

2 cups bean sprouts

PUD PUK SAI MOO
pork with vegetables

Heat the oil in a wok and cook the rice noodles, in batches, for 15–20 seconds, or until they puff up. Remove with a slotted spoon, drain on paper towels, and set aside.

Pour off all but 2 tablespoons of the oil and stir-fry the pork, onion, garlic, gingerroot, and chili for 4–5 minutes, or until the meat has browned.

Add the corn cobs, red bell pepper, and broccoli and stir-fry for 3–4 minutes, or until the vegetables are just tender. Stir in the black bean sauce and bean sprouts, then cook for another 2–3 minutes. Serve immediately, topped with the crispy noodles.

MAKES 16

12 oz/350 g ground pork

2 tbsp finely chopped fresh cilantro

1 garlic clove, crushed

1 fresh green chili, seeded and chopped

3 tbsp cornstarch

1 egg white

½ tsp salt

16 won ton wrappers

1 tbsp water

vegetable oil or peanut oil, for
  deep-frying

chili sauce, to serve

MOO KROB

crispy pork won tons

Put the pork in a bowl and beat in the cilantro, garlic, chili, 1 tablespoon of the cornstarch, the egg white, and salt. Beat together to a thick, smooth texture. With damp hands, shape into 16 equal portions and roll into balls.

Put a pork ball in the center of each won ton wrapper. Make a paste by mixing the remaining cornstarch with 1 tablespoon of water. Brush the edges of the wrappers with the cornstarch paste and gather them up around the filling to make half into small, sacklike parcels, and the rest into triangular shapes.

Arrange the won tons in a single layer (in batches if need be) in the top of a steamer and cook over boiling water for 10–15 minutes, or until the meat is cooked through.

Heat enough oil for deep-frying in a wok, deep-fat fryer, or large, heavy-bottomed pan until it reaches 350–375°F/180–190°C, or until a cube of bread browns in 30 seconds. Carefully drop the won tons into the oil and deep-fry for 2–3 minutes, or until golden brown and crisp. Drain on paper towels and serve hot with chili sauce.

SERVES 4

10 oz/280 g pork side

1 tbsp vegetable oil or peanut oil

1 tbsp chili bean sauce

1 tbsp fermented black beans, rinsed
and lightly mashed

1 tsp sweet red bean paste (optional)

1 tsp sugar

1 tsp dark soy sauce

pinch of white pepper

1 green bell pepper, cored, seeded,
and thinly sliced

1 red bell pepper, cored, seeded, and
thinly sliced

WUI WO YUK
spicy sichuan pork

Bring a pan of water to a boil, place the pork in the pan, cover, and simmer for about 20 minutes, skimming occasionally. Let the pork cool and rest before slicing thinly.

In a preheated wok or deep pan, heat the oil and stir-fry the pork slices until they begin to shrink. Stir in the chili bean sauce, then add the black beans, and then the sweet red bean paste (if using), and the sugar, dark soy sauce, and white pepper. Finally, toss in the bell peppers and stir-fry for a couple of minutes.

COOK'S TIP
Use Chinese leeks instead of bell peppers, if available. Take 2 leeks and thinly slice them diagonally.

SERVES 4

1 tbsp vegetable oil or peanut oil

1 tbsp chili oil

1 lb/450 g pork tenderloin, thinly sliced

2 tbsp green chili sauce

6 scallions, sliced

1-inch/2.5-cm piece fresh gingerroot, thinly sliced

1 red bell pepper, cored, seeded, and sliced

1 yellow bell pepper, cored, seeded, and sliced

1 orange bell pepper, cored, seeded, and sliced

1 tbsp Thai fish sauce

2 tbsp Thai soy sauce

juice of ½ lime

4 tbsp chopped fresh parsley

cooked flat rice noodles, to serve

PUD MOO PHRIK-THAI
pork with bell peppers

Heat both the oils in a wok. Add the pork, in batches, and stir-fry until browned all over. Remove with a slotted spoon and reserve.

Add the chili sauce, scallions, and gingerroot to the wok and stir-fry for 1–2 minutes. Add the bell peppers and stir–fry for 2–3 minutes.

Return the meat to the wok, stir well, and add the fish sauce, soy sauce, and lime juice. Cook for another 1–2 minutes, then stir in the parsley and serve with flat rice noodles.

SERVES 4

1½ cups plain yogurt

½ tsp ground asafetida dissolved in
2 tbsp water

1 lb 9 oz/700 g boneless leg of lamb,
trimmed and cut into 2-inch/5-cm cubes

2 tomatoes, seeded and chopped

1 onion, chopped

2 tbsp ghee, vegetable oil, or peanut oil

1½ tbsp Garlic and Ginger Paste

2 tbsp tomato paste

2 fresh bay leaves, plus extra to garnish

1 tbsp ground coriander

¼–1 tsp chili powder

½ tsp ground turmeric

1 tsp salt

½ tsp garam masala

ROGAN JOSH

rogan josh

Put the yogurt in a large bowl and stir in the dissolved asafetida. Add the lamb and use your hands to rub in all the marinade, then set aside for 30 minutes.

Meanwhile, put the tomatoes and onion in a blender and whizz until blended. Melt the ghee in a flameproof casserole or large skillet with a tight-fitting lid. Add the garlic and ginger paste and stir around until you can smell cooked garlic.

Stir in the tomato mixture, tomato paste, bay leaves, coriander, chili powder, and turmeric, then reduce the heat to low and simmer, stirring occasionally, for 5–8 minutes.

Add the lamb and salt, with any leftover marinade, and stir around for 2 minutes. Cover, reduce the heat to low, and simmer, stirring occasionally, for 30 minutes. The lamb should give off enough moisture to prevent it from catching on the bottom of the pan, but if the sauce looks too dry, stir in a little water.

Sprinkle the lamb with the garam masala, replace the lid on the pan, and continue simmering for 15–20 minutes, or until the lamb is tender when pierced with a fork. Adjust the seasoning, if necessary. Remove from the heat and serve garnished with bay leaves.

COOK'S TIP
For an authentic flavor, search out the bright-red Kashmiri chili powder sold at Asian food stores.

SERVES 4–6

4 large onions, 2 thinly sliced and
    2 coarsely chopped
1½ tsp salt
2 tbsp Garlic and Ginger Paste
½ tsp ground paprika
2 tbsp chopped fresh cilantro
1 tbsp ground coriander
1 tsp ground cumin

½ tsp ground asafetida
5 tbsp ghee, vegetable oil, or peanut oil
1 lb 9 oz/700 g boneless shoulder of
    lamb, trimmed and cut into 2-inch/
    5-cm cubes
4 green cardamom pods
pinch of sugar
½ tsp garam masala
few sprigs of fresh cilantro, to garnish

GOSHT DOPIAZA
lamb dopiaza

Put the 2 sliced onions in a bowl, sprinkle with 1 teaspoon of the salt, and let stand for about 5 minutes to extract the moisture. Use your hands to squeeze out the moisture.

Meanwhile, grind the 2 chopped onions with the garlic and ginger paste, paprika, fresh cilantro, ground coriander, the cumin, and asafetida in a spice blender or using a pestle and mortar.

Melt 2 tablespoons of the ghee in a flameproof casserole or skillet with a tight-fitting lid over medium-high heat. Add the sliced onions and cook, stirring constantly, for 4–6 minutes, until golden. Immediately tip them out of the pan; they will continue to darken as they cool (if you wait until they are brown, they will develop a burnt taste).

Melt 2 tablespoons of the remaining ghee in the casserole. Add the lamb and cook to brown on all sides, working in batches if necessary, then remove from the pan.

Melt the remaining ghee in the casserole. Add the onion paste and cook, stirring occasionally. Add the cardamom and stir. Return the lamb to the casserole; stir in the sugar and the remaining ½ teaspoon salt. Reduce the heat to very low and simmer, covered, for 30 minutes.

Uncover the casserole and sprinkle the reserved onion slices and the garam masala over the lamb, replace the lid on the pan, and simmer for another 15 minutes, or until the lamb is tender. Taste and adjust the seasoning, if necessary. Sprinkle with cilantro sprigs, and serve.

Fish and Shellfish

SERVES 4

2 tbsp vegetable oil or peanut oil

1 large onion, chopped

2 garlic cloves, chopped

3 oz/85 g white mushrooms

8 oz/225 g angler fish, cut into cubes,
each about 1 inch/2.5 cm

8 oz/225 g salmon fillets, cut into cubes,
each about 1 inch/2.5 cm

8 oz/225 g cod fillet, cut into cubes,
each about 1 inch/2.5 cm

2 tbsp Thai red curry paste

14 oz/400 g canned coconut milk

3–4 tbsp chopped fresh cilantro

1 tsp jaggery or soft, light
brown sugar

1 tsp Thai fish sauce

4 oz/115 g rice noodles

3 scallions, chopped

1 cup bean sprouts

few fresh Thai basil leaves, plus sprigs
to garnish

GUAY TIAW KAENG PLA
fish curry with rice noodles

Heat the oil in a wok or large skillet and gently cook the onion, garlic, and mushrooms, until softened but not browned.

Add the fish, curry paste, and coconut milk and bring gently to a boil. Simmer for 2–3 minutes before adding half the cilantro, the jaggery, and fish sauce. Keep warm.

Meanwhile, soak the noodles for 3–4 minutes (check the package instructions) or until tender, then drain well through a colander. Put the colander and noodles over a pan of simmering water. Add the scallions, bean sprouts, and basil leaves and steam on top of the noodles for 1–2 minutes, or until just wilted.

Pile the noodles onto warmed serving plates and top with the fish curry. Scatter the remaining cilantro and the basil sprigs over the top and serve immediately.

SERVES 4–6

2 lb/900 g thick fish fillets, such as
   angler fish, red snapper, cod, or
   haddock, rinsed and cut into
   large chunks

2 bay leaves, torn

⅔ cup ghee, vegetable oil, or peanut oil

2 large onions, chopped

½ tbsp salt

⅔ cup water

sprigs of fresh cilantro, to garnish

MARINADE

½ tbsp Garlic and Ginger Paste

1 fresh green chili, seeded and chopped

1 tsp ground coriander

1 tsp ground cumin

½ tsp ground turmeric

¼–½ tsp chili powder

salt

1 tbsp water

MACHCHLI MASALA
balti fish curry

To make the marinade, mix the garlic and ginger paste, green chili, ground coriander, cumin, turmeric, and chili powder together with salt to taste in a large bowl. Gradually stir in the water to form a thin paste. Add the fish chunks and smear with the marinade. Tuck the bay leaves underneath, cover with plastic wrap, and let marinate in the refrigerator for at least 30 minutes, or up to 4 hours.

When you are ready to cook the fish, remove from the refrigerator 15 minutes in advance. Melt the ghee in a wok or large skillet over medium-high heat. Add the onions, sprinkle with the salt, and cook, stirring frequently, for 8 minutes, or until it is very soft and golden.

Gently add the fish and bay leaves to the pan and stir in the water. Bring to a boil, then immediately lower the heat and cook the fish for 4–5 minutes, spooning the sauce over the fish and carefully moving the chunks around, until they are cooked through and the flesh flakes easily. Adjust the seasoning, if necessary. Remove from the heat, discard the bay leaves, and sprinkle with cilantro.

COOK'S TIP
Do not overbrown the onions, or the dish will taste bitter. They should be golden, but not brown, when the fish is added.

SERVES 4

4 angler fish fillets, about 4 oz/115 g each

generous 2 tbsp rice flour or cornstarch

6 tbsp vegetable oil or peanut oil

4 garlic cloves, crushed

2 large fresh red chilies, seeded
and sliced

2 tsp jaggery or soft, light brown sugar

juice of 2 limes

grated zest of 1 lime

TO SERVE

boiled rice

lime wedges

YUM PLA

101

angler fish with lime and chili sauce

Toss the fish in the flour, shaking off any excess. Heat the oil in a wok and cook the fish on all sides until browned and cooked through, taking care when turning not to break it up.

Lift the fish out of the wok and keep it warm. Add the garlic and chilies to the pan and stir-fry for 1–2 minutes, or until they have softened.

Add the jaggery, the lime juice and zest, and 2–3 tablespoons of water and bring to a boil. Simmer gently for 1–2 minutes, then spoon the mixture over the fish. Serve immediately, with boiled rice and some lime wedges.

SERVES 4–6

½ tsp salt

2 tbsp lemon juice or distilled
   white vinegar

1 lb 9 oz/700 g skinless white fish
   fillets, such as cod, halibut, or angler
   fish, rinsed, patted dry, and
   cut into large chunks

vegetable oil or peanut oil, for
   deep-frying

pepper

lemon wedges, to serve

BATTER

1 cup besan or gram flour

seeds from 4 green cardamom pods

large pinch of ground turmeric

large pinch of baking soda

finely grated zest of 1 lemon

¾ cup water

salt and pepper

102 MACHCHLI PAKORA
fish pakoras

Combine the salt, lemon juice, and pepper to taste and rub all over the fish chunks, then set aside in a nonmetallic bowl and let stand for 20–30 minutes.

Meanwhile, to make the batter, put the besan flour in a bowl and stir in the seeds from the cardamom pods, the turmeric, baking soda, and lemon zest, and salt and pepper to taste. Make a well in the center and gradually stir in the water until a thin batter similar to light cream forms.

Gently stir the pieces of fish into the batter, taking care not to break them up.

Heat enough oil for deep-frying in a wok, deep-fat fryer, or large, heavy-bottomed pan to 350–375°F/180–190°C, or until a cube of bread browns in 30 seconds. Remove the fish pieces from the batter and let the excess batter drip back into the bowl. Without overcrowding the pan, drop fish pieces in the hot fat and cook for 2½–3 minutes, or until golden brown.

Immediately use a slotted spoon to remove the cooked fish pieces from the fat and drain on crumpled paper towels. Continue until all the fish is cooked, then serve hot with the lemon wedges for squeezing over.

COOK'S TIP
The batter can be made several hours in advance and set aside, covered with plastic wrap. Stir it well before using and add a little extra water if it has become too thick. If the batter is too thick, it will remain raw next to the fish.

SERVES 4

1 lb/450 g angler fish or cod
  fillets, cubed

8 oz/225 g salmon fillets, cubed

4 oz/115 g wide rice noodles

2 tbsp vegetable oil or peanut oil

2 shallots, sliced

2 garlic cloves, finely chopped

1 fresh red chili, seeded and chopped

2 tbsp Thai soy sauce

2 tbsp chili sauce

sprigs of fresh cilantro, to garnish

MARINADE

2 tbsp vegetable oil or peanut oil

2 fresh green chilies, seeded
  and chopped

grated zest and juice of 1 lime

1 tbsp Thai fish sauce

104 GUAY TIAW PLA
stir-fried rice noodles with marinated fish

Place the fish in a shallow bowl. Mix the marinade ingredients together and pour over the fish. Cover with plastic wrap and chill for 2 hours.

Put the noodles in a bowl and cover with boiling water. Let stand for 8–10 minutes (check the package instructions) and drain well.

Heat the oil in a wok or large skillet and cook the shallots, garlic, and red chili until lightly browned. Add the soy sauce and chili sauce. Add the fish and the marinade to the wok and stir-fry gently for 2–3 minutes, or until cooked through.

Add the drained noodles and stir gently. Garnish with fresh cilantro sprigs and serve immediately.

SERVES 4–6

1 whole sea bass or similar, weighing
  1–1½ lb/450–675 g, scaled and gutted

½ tsp salt

2-inch/5-cm piece of fresh
  gingerroot, julienned

1 tsp Shaoxing rice wine

1 tbsp slivered scallion

1 tbsp vegetable oil or peanut oil

1 tbsp light soy sauce

CHING JING YU

cantonese steamed fish

To prepare the fish, clean and dry thoroughly. Score the fish on both sides with deep, diagonal cuts. Press the salt into the skin and set aside for 20 minutes.

Place the fish on a plate and top with the gingerroot, Shaoxing, and half the scallion. Steam in a steamer for 8–10 minutes.

Heat the oil in a small pan until smoking and cook the remaining scallion. Arrange this over the fish, pour over the light soy sauce, and serve.

COOK'S TIP
In China, fish is always served very fresh, complete with tail and head. The fish cheeks are reserved for the most important guest at a meal and are believed to be the sweetest and best part of the fish.

SERVES 4

1 quantity Cilantro Chutney

1 large fresh banana leaf

vegetable oil or peanut oil, for brushing

4 white fish fillets, such as butterfish
or flounder, about 5 oz/140 g each

salt and pepper

lime or lemon wedges, to serve

PAATRANI MACHCHI
steamed fish with cilantro chutney

Prepare the Coriander Chutney at least 2 hours in advance to let the flavors blend.

Cut the banana leaf into 4 squares large enough to fold around the fish to make tight packets, about 10 inches/25 cm square. Working with one piece of leaf at a time, lightly rub the bottom with oil. Put one of the fish fillets in the center of the oiled side, flesh-side up. Spread one fourth of the coriander chutney over the top and season to taste.

Fold one side of the leaf over the fish, then fold the opposite side over. Turn the leaf so the folded edges are top and bottom. Fold the right-hand end of the leaf packet into the center, then fold over the left-hand side. Use 2 wooden skewers to close the packet. Repeat with the remaining ingredients. The packets can now be refrigerated for several hours.

Place a steamer large enough to hold the packets in a single layer over a pan of boiling water, without letting the water touch the fish. Add the fish, cover the pan, and steam for 15 minutes. Open 1 packet to test that the fish is cooked through and flakes easily. Serve the packets wrapped, with lime or lemon wedges, and let each guest open his or her own to release the aromas.

COOK'S TIP
Fresh banana leaves are sold in many Asian food stores. If you can't find banana leaves, use kitchen foil, shiny-side up, sealing the edges tightly.

SERVES 3–4

1 flounder, gutted

½ tsp salt

2 tsp fermented black beans, rinsed
   and chopped

2 tsp finely chopped garlic

1 tsp finely shredded fresh gingerroot

1 tbsp shredded scallion

1 tbsp light soy sauce

1 tsp Shaoxing rice wine

1 tsp vegetable oil or peanut oil

dash of sesame oil

½ tsp sugar

pinch of white pepper

110 SI JAP JIN TAAP SA

steamed flounder with black bean sauce

Place the fish on a plate that fits into your steamer or create a small dish with foil. Put all the other ingredients on top of the fish. Place in a steamer for 10–12 minutes, or until the fish is cooked. Serve immediately.

VARIATION
Any white fish is suitable for this dish, and frozen fish can also be used. Make sure the fish fits into your steamer.

SERVES 4

4 tbsp vegetable oil or peanut oil,
  plus extra for brushing

finely grated zest and juice of 1 lime

4 large mackerel filets, about
  6 oz/175 g each

1½ tsp cumin seeds

1½ tsp black mustard seeds

1½ tsp nigella seeds

1½ tsp fennel seeds

1½ tsp coriander seeds

1½-inch/4-cm piece fresh gingerroot,
  very finely chopped

1½ garlic cloves, very finely chopped

3 shallots, very finely chopped

pinch of chili powder

salt and pepper

fresh red chilies, seeded and very finely
  sliced, to garnish

lime wedges, to serve

BHANGDE LONCHEN
pickled mackerel

Mix together 2 tablespoons of the oil with the lime zest and juice, and salt and pepper to taste, in a nonmetallic bowl that will hold the mackerel fillets in a flat layer. Add the mackerel fillets and use your hands to cover them in the marinade, then set aside for at least 10 minutes, or cover with plastic wrap and chill for up to 4 hours.

When you are ready to cook the fish, preheat the broiler to high, and lightly brush the broiler pan with oil.

Remove the mackerel from the refrigerator 15 minutes in advance. Put the mackerel on the broiler pan, skin-side down, and broil about 4 inches/10 cm from the source of the heat for 6 minutes, or until the flesh appears cooked through when pierced with the tip of a knife and flakes easily.

While the mackerel is cooking, heat the remaining 2 tablespoons of oil in a wok or large skillet over medium-high heat. Add the cumin, black mustard seeds, nigella, fennel, and coriander seeds, and stir around, until the black mustard seeds start to jump and the coriander and cumin seeds just start to brown. Immediately remove the pan from the heat and stir in the gingerroot, garlic, shallots, and chili powder, then continue stirring for 1 minute.

Transfer the mackerel fillets to plates and spoon the spice mixture over. Garnish with red chili slices and serve with lime wedges for squeezing over.

VARIATION
The spicy flavor of this recipe works well with any oily fish fillets, so try herring, salmon, and tuna as well.

SERVES 4–6

1 whole freshwater fish, such as trout
   or carp, weighing 14 oz/400 g, gutted

1 heaping tbsp all-purpose flour

pinch of salt

scant ½ cup water

vegetable oil or peanut oil, for
   deep-frying

SAUCE

scant ½ cup vegetable oil or peanut oil

1 tsp dried chili flakes

1 garlic clove, finely chopped

1 tsp finely chopped fresh gingerroot

1 tbsp chili bean sauce

½ tsp white pepper

2 tsp sugar

1 tbsp white rice vinegar

1 tsp finely chopped scallion

114 DAU FAAN YU
deep-fried river fish with chili bean sauce

To prepare the fish, clean and dry thoroughly. Mix together the flour, salt, and water to create a light batter. Coat the fish with the batter.

Heat enough oil for deep-frying in a wok, deep-fat fryer, or large, heavy-bottomed pan, until it reaches 350–375°F/180–190°C, or until a cube of bread browns in 30 seconds. Deep-fry the fish on one side at a time, until the skin is crisp and golden brown. Drain, set aside, and keep warm.

To make the sauce, first heat all but 1 tablespoon of the oil in a small pan and, when smoking, pour over the dried chili flakes in a heatproof bowl. Set aside.

In a preheated wok or deep pan, heat the remaining oil and stir-fry the garlic and gingerroot until fragrant. Stir in the chili bean sauce, then add the oil-chili flake mixture. Season with the pepper, sugar, and vinegar. Turn off the heat and stir in the scallion. Spoon over the fish and serve immediately.

SERVES 4

2 tbsp vegetable oil or peanut oil

3 shallots, finely chopped

2 garlic cloves, finely chopped

generous 1 cup jasmine rice

1¼ cups fish bouillon

4 scallions, chopped

2 tbsp Thai red curry paste

8 oz/225 g baby squid, cleaned
  and thickly sliced

8 oz/225 g white fish fillets, skinned
  and cut into cubes

8 oz/225 g salmon fillets, skinned
  and cut into cubes

4 tbsp chopped fresh cilantro

116 KHAO SAI KHUNG LA PHA-MUK

rice with seafood and squid

Heat 1 tablespoon of the oil in a wok and stir-fry the shallots and garlic for 2–3 minutes, or until softened. Add the rice and stir-fry for 2–3 minutes.

Add a ladleful of the bouillon and simmer, adding more bouillon as needed, for 12–15 minutes, or until tender. Transfer to a dish, cool, cover with plastic wrap, and chill overnight.

Heat the remaining oil in a wok and stir-fry the scallions and curry paste for 2–3 minutes. Add the squid and fish cubes and stir-fry gently to avoid breaking up the fish. Stir in the rice and cilantro, heat through gently, and serve.

SERVES 4–6

1 tbsp vegetable oil or peanut oil

4 oz/115 g raw shrimp, peeled
  and deveined

4 eggs, lightly beaten

1 tsp salt

pinch of white pepper

2 tbsp finely chopped fresh
  Chinese chives

FU YUNG HA
shrimp fu yung

In a preheated wok or skillet, heat the oil and stir-fry the shrimp until they begin to turn pink.

Season the beaten eggs with the salt and pepper and pour over the shrimp. Stir-fry for 1 minute, then add the chives.

Cook for another 4 minutes, stirring all the time, until the eggs are cooked through but still soft in texture, and serve immediately.

COOK'S TIP
Chinese chives are also known as garlic chives and have quite a subtle flavor.

SERVES 4

1 lb/450 g raw jumbo shrimp

1 tbsp vegetable oil or peanut oil

3 shallots, finely chopped

2 garlic cloves, finely chopped

1-inch/2.5-cm piece fresh gingerroot,
thinly sliced

1¾ cups canned coconut milk

1 tbsp Thai green curry paste

3–4 fresh Thai basil leaves

1 tsp jaggery or soft, light
brown sugar

8 oz/225 g flat rice noodles

2 tsp sesame oil

2 tbsp sesame seeds, toasted

few sprigs of fresh Thai basil, to garnish

4 cooked unpeeled jumbo shrimp,
to garnish

GUAY TIAW KUNG
shrimp with noodles

120

Peel the shrimp, removing and discarding the heads. Cut a slit along the back of each and remove and discard the dark vein.

Heat the oil in a wok and stir-fry the shallots, garlic, and gingerroot for 2–3 minutes. Add the coconut milk and curry paste and simmer for 2–3 minutes.

Add the shrimp, basil leaves, and jaggery and cook until the shrimp turns pink.

Meanwhile, cook the noodles in boiling water according to the package instructions, then drain well. Stir in the sesame oil and seeds and serve immediately with the shrimp, garnished with the sprigs of basil and unpeeled shrimp.

SERVES 4–6

4 oz/115 g pork loin

1 tbsp honey, dissolved in 1 tsp boiling water

10½ oz/300 g thin rice vermicelli

3 tbsp vegetable oil or peanut oil

2 garlic cloves, finely chopped

1 lb 2 oz/500 g small raw shrimp, peeled, deveined, and chopped into 2–3 pieces each

1 onion, finely sliced

1 tbsp mild curry powder, such as garam masala

1 green bell pepper, cored, seeded, and thinly sliced

1 tsp sugar

1 tsp salt

1–2 tsp chicken bouillon

1 tbsp light soy sauce

3½ cups bean sprouts, trimmed

CHA SIU MARINADE

1 tsp yellow bean sauce, lightly crushed

1 tsp red fermented bean curd

1 tsp Peking sauce

1 tsp oyster sauce

1 tsp dark soy sauce

1 tsp sugar

2 tsp Shaoxing rice wine

½ tsp sesame oil

SING JAU CHAAU MAI
singapore noodles

Combine all the marinade ingredients. Cut the pork loin lengthwise into 2 pieces. Arrange in a single layer in a dish and pour the marinade over the top. Cover with plastic wrap and marinate for at least 2 hours, basting occasionally.

Preheat the oven to 425°F/220°C. On a wire cooling rack, lay out the pieces of pork in a single layer, reserving the marinade. Place the rack over a dish of boiling water and bake for about 15 minutes, ensuring that there is always a little water in the pan.

Reduce the oven temperature to 350°F/180°C. Turn the pork over and baste with the marinade. Cook for another 10 minutes.

Remove from the oven and preheat the broiler. Brush the pork with the honey and place under the broiler for a few minutes, turning once. Let cool, then cut into julienne strips.

Meanwhile, cook the rice vermicelli according to the instructions on the package. Drain and set aside.

In a preheated wok, heat 2 tablespoons of the oil. Add the garlic and stir-fry until fragrant. Add the shrimp and stir-fry for 1 minute, or until beginning to change color. Add the reserved cha siu and stir-fry for 1 minute. Remove everything from the wok and set aside.

Clean your wok and heat the remaining oil. Add the onion and stir-fry for 1 minute, then stir in the curry powder. Add the bell pepper, sugar, salt, and bouillon, and stir-fry for 2 minutes. Pour in the light soy sauce, then add the rice vermicelli. Toss well. Finally, add the bean sprouts and the shrimp and pork. Stir until warmed through, then serve immediately.

SERVES 6

2 tsp coriander seeds

½ tsp black peppercorns

1 large garlic clove, crushed

1 tsp ground turmeric

¼–½ tsp chili powder

½ tsp salt

3 tbsp ghee, vegetable oil, or peanut oil

1 onion, grated

1 lb 12 oz/800 g canned
   chopped tomatoes

pinch of sugar

1 lb 2 oz/500 g small, cooked, peeled
   shrimp, thawed if frozen

½ tsp garam masala, plus extra
   to garnish

6 Pooris, warmed

fresh cilantro, chopped, to garnish

JHINGA PURI
shrimp pooris

Put the coriander seeds, peppercorns, garlic, turmeric, chili powder, and salt in a small food processor or spice grinder, or use a pestle and mortar to blend to a thick paste.

Melt the ghee in a wok or large skillet over medium-low heat. Add the spicy paste and cook, stirring constantly, for about 30 seconds.

Add the grated onion and stir for another 30 seconds. Stir in the tomatoes with their juice and the sugar. Bring to a boil, stirring, and let bubble for 10 minutes, mashing the tomatoes against the side of the pan to break them down, or until reduced. Taste and add extra salt, if necessary.

Add the shrimp and sprinkle with the garam masala. When the shrimp are hot, arrange the hot pooris on plates and top each one with a portion of the shrimp. Sprinkle with the cilantro and more garam masala.

COOK'S TIP

Deep-fried Pooris are best served straight from the pan, so it is a good idea to have a couple of pans to use if you are entertaining. The Pooris, with their rich, light texture, are traditional with this dish, but chapatis or nans are also good, especially if you want to avoid last-minute deep-frying.

SERVES 4

3 tbsp vegetable oil or peanut oil

2 large fresh crabs, cleaned, broken into pieces, and legs cracked with a cleaver

2 oz/55 g fresh gingerroot, julienned

3½ oz/100 g scallions, chopped into 2-inch/5-cm lengths

2 tbsp light soy sauce

1 tsp sugar

pinch of white pepper

GEUNG CHUNG CHAAU HAI
stir-fried fresh crab with ginger

In a preheated wok or deep pan, heat 2 tablespoons of the oil and cook the crab over high heat for 3–4 minutes. Remove and set aside.

Clean your wok or pan and heat the remaining oil, toss in the gingerroot and stir until fragrant. Add the scallions, then stir in the crab pieces. Add the light soy sauce, sugar, and white pepper. Cover and simmer for 1 minute and serve immediately.

COOK'S TIP

This dish can be made only with whole fresh crabs, whether from the sea or freshwater.

SERVES 4

3 tbsp vegetable oil or peanut oil

½ tbsp black mustard seeds

8 shallots, chopped

2 garlic cloves, crushed

2 tbsp distilled vinegar

4 small, fresh, red chilies

1¼ cups coconut cream

10 fresh curry leaves or 1 tbsp dried

½ tsp ground turmeric

¼–½ tsp chili powder

4 lb 8 oz/2 kg live mussels, scrubbed
and debearded

salt

TISSARIO KADUGU
mussels with mustard seeds and shallots

Heat the oil in a wok or large skillet over medium-high heat. Add the mustard seeds and stir them around for 1 minute, or until they start to jump.

Add the shallots and garlic cloves and cook, stirring frequently, for 3 minutes, or until they start to brown. Stir in the vinegar, whole chilies, coconut cream, the curry leaves, turmeric, chili powder, and a pinch of salt and bring to a boil, stirring.

Reduce the heat to very low. Add the mussels, cover the pan, and let the mussels simmer, shaking the pan frequently, for 3–4 minutes, or until they are all open. Discard any that remain closed. Ladle the mussels into deep bowls, then taste the broth and add extra salt, if necessary. Spoon over the mussels and serve.

COOK'S TIP
Taste the bright yellow broth before you add it to the mussels. If the mussels are gritty, strain the liquid through a strainer lined with cheesecloth or paper towels. Mussels should be cooked on the day of purchase. When live mussels don't close or cooked ones don't open, it is an indication that they aren't fresh or that they are dead. They must not be eaten.

SERVES 4

2 tbsp vegetable oil or peanut oil

1 tsp finely chopped garlic

1 tsp finely chopped fresh gingerroot

1 tbsp fermented black beans, rinsed
and lightly mashed

14 oz/400 g scallops, shelled

½ tsp light soy sauce

1 tsp Shaoxing rice wine

1 tsp sugar

3–4 fresh red bird's-eye chilies,
finely chopped

1–2 tsp chicken bouillon (optional)

1 tbsp finely chopped scallion

SI JAP CHAAU DAI JI
scallops in black bean sauce

Heat the oil in a preheated wok or deep pan. Add the garlic and stir, then add the gingerroot and stir-fry together for 1 minute, or until fragrant. Mix in the black beans, toss in the scallops, and stir-fry for 1 minute. Add the light soy sauce, Shaoxing, sugar, and chilies.

Lower the heat and simmer for 2 minutes, adding the bouillon if necessary. Finally, add the scallion, stir, and serve.

COOK'S TIP
Fresh scallops, removed from their shells, are always preferable, but thawed frozen scallops work well in this strongly flavored dish.

SERVES 4

SPICE PASTE

2 tbsp vegetable oil or peanut oil

1 tbsp chili oil with shrimp

2 shallots, chopped

2–3 large, fresh, red chilies, seeded and
   coarsely chopped

2 tbsp ground coriander

2 tbsp ground cumin

1-inch/2.5-cm piece fresh
   gingerroot, chopped

1 tbsp finely chopped lemongrass

3–4 cilantro roots, chopped

1 tsp salt

1 tsp jaggery or soft, light
   brown sugar

STIR-FRY

2 red bell peppers, cored, seeded,
   and diced

⅔ cup plain yogurt

1 lb 10 oz/750 g squid, cleaned and sliced

juice of 1 lime

⅔ cup coconut cream

PUD PLA-MUK SAI PHRIK-DEANG
squid and red bell peppers

Put all the ingredients for the Spice Paste into a food processor and process until finely chopped.

Scrape the paste into a wok and stir-fry gently for 3–4 minutes. Add the red bell peppers and stir-fry for 1–2 minutes.

Add the yogurt and bring to a boil. Add the squid and simmer for 2–3 minutes, then stir in the lime juice and coconut cream. Simmer for another 1–2 minutes. Serve immediately.

Vegetarian

SERVES 4–6

8 oz/225 g soft bean curd (drained
   weight), cut into ½-inch/1-cm cubes

4 eggs, beaten

pinch of salt

3½ oz/100 g Chinese chives,
   finely chopped

1 tbsp Shaoxing rice wine

3 tbsp vegetable oil or peanut oil

4–5 tbsp vegetable bouillon

WAAT DAAN DAU FU
scrambled eggs with bean curd

Drop the bean curd into a large pan of boiling water and cook for 2 minutes. Drain and set aside.

Combine the eggs with the salt, half the chopped chives, and 1 teaspoon of the Shaoxing.

In a preheated wok or large pan, heat 2 tablespoons of the oil, add the eggs, and stir rapidly for 2 minutes, or until the eggs are scrambled. Remove from the heat and set aside.

Clean your wok or pan and heat the remaining oil and stir-fry the bean curd cubes for 2 minutes. Add the bouillon and remaining Shaoxing and simmer for 3 minutes. Add the scrambled eggs and remaining chives and stir. Serve immediately.

COOK'S TIP
Nonvegetarians might prefer to use chicken bouillon.

MAKES 8

3 tbsp mustard oil

2 tsp black mustard seeds

12 fresh curry leaves or 1 tbsp dried

3 fresh green chilies, seeded and chopped

1½ large onions, chopped

½ tsp ground turmeric

1 lb 10 oz/750 g new potatoes,
   scrubbed and chopped

scant 2 cups water

½–1 tbsp tamarind paste

2 tbsp coconut cream

fresh cilantro, chopped

8 Dosas, kept warm

salt

selection of chutneys, to serve

MASALA DOSA
dosa masala

Heat the mustard oil in a large skillet or pan with a lid over high heat, until it smokes. Turn off the heat and let the mustard oil cool completely.

Reheat the mustard oil over medium-high heat. Add the mustard seeds and stir until they start to jump. Stir in the curry leaves, chilies, and onions and cook, stirring frequently, for 5–8 minutes, or until the onions are soft but not brown.

Stir in the turmeric, then add the potatoes and a pinch of salt. Pour in the water and bring to a boil. Reduce the heat to the lowest setting and simmer, covered, for 12–15 minutes, or until the potatoes are very tender and almost falling apart, and most of the water has evaporated. Stir in the tamarind paste and coconut—add extra, if necessary—then stir in the cilantro.

One side of each dosa will be a smooth golden brown and the other side will be more mottled. Put one-eighth of the filling on the mottled side and roll the dosa around it. Continue until all the dosas are filled. Serve hot or at room temperature with a selection of chutneys.

COOK'S TIP
Vegetable oil or peanut oil can replace the mustard oil. If you make this replacement, skip the first step.

SERVES 4–6

3 dried Chinese mushrooms, soaked in
warm water for 20 minutes

2 oz/55 g baby bok choy

vegetable oil or peanut oil, for
deep-frying

1 lb/450 g firm bean curd, cut into
1-inch/2.5-cm squares

2 oz/55 g fresh or canned bamboo
shoots, rinsed and finely sliced
(if using fresh shoots, boil in
water first for 30 minutes)

1 tsp oyster sauce

1 tsp light soy sauce

SEUN JIM DAU FU
bamboo shoots
with bean curd

Squeeze out any excess water from the mushrooms and thinly slice, discarding any tough stems. Blanch the bok choy in a large pan of boiling water for 30 seconds. Drain and set aside.

Heat enough oil for deep-frying in a wok, deep-fat fryer, or large, heavy-bottomed pan, until it reaches 350–375°F/180–190°C, or until a cube of bread browns in 30 seconds. Cook the bean curd cubes until golden brown. Remove, drain, and set aside.

In a preheated wok or deep pan, heat 1 tablespoon of the oil, toss in the mushrooms and bok choy, and stir. Add the bean curd and bamboo shoots with the oyster and soy sauces. Heat through and serve.

SERVES 4

2 tbsp vegetable oil or peanut oil

6 scallions, sliced

1 tbsp Thai green curry paste

4 oz/115 g shiitake mushrooms, halved

4 oz/115 g oyster mushrooms

4 oz/115 g white mushrooms

4 oz/115 g portobello mushrooms, sliced

2 tbsp Thai soy sauce

1 tsp jaggery or soft, light brown sugar

8 oz/225 g canned water chestnuts, drained, rinsed, and sliced

1 cup bean sprouts

cooked noodles, to serve

142 PUD HED RUEM
mixed mushroom stir-fry

Heat the oil in a wok or skillet and stir-fry the scallions for 30 seconds. Add the curry paste and stir-fry for 1–2 minutes. Add all the mushrooms and stir-fry over high heat, until they are tender.

Add the soy sauce, jaggery, water chestnuts, and bean sprouts and cook for 1–2 minutes, or until heated through and just tender. Serve hot with cooked noodles.

SERVES 4–6

14 oz/400 g thin wheat-flour noodles

2½ cups bean sprouts, trimmed

1 tbsp very finely chopped scallion,
   to garnish

SESAME SAUCE

1 tbsp sugar

1 tbsp sesame oil

¼ cup sesame paste

1 tbsp chili oil

2 tsp dark soy sauce

1 tbsp black Chinese vinegar

144 SING DOU MA LAAT MIN

chengdu noodles in sesame sauce

Cook the noodles according to the instructions on the package. When cooked, rinse under cold water and set aside. Blanch the bean sprouts in a large pan of boiling water for 30 seconds. Drain and set aside.

To prepare the Sesame Sauce, beat all the ingredients together, until the sauce is smooth and thick.

To serve, toss the noodles in the sauce, stir in the bean sprouts, and sprinkle with chopped scallion.

COOK'S TIP
Vary the proportions of the sauce ingredients for an even stronger or spicier flavor.

VEGETARIAN

SERVES 4–6

2 eggs

½ tsp salt

pinch of white pepper

1 tsp unsalted butter

2 tbsp vegetable oil or peanut oil

1 tsp finely chopped garlic

1 small onion, finely sliced

1 green bell pepper, cored, seeded,
  and thinly sliced

1 lb/450 g cooked rice, chilled

1 tbsp light soy sauce

1 tbsp finely chopped scallion

2½ cups sprouts, trimmed

2 drops of sesame oil

FU YUNG DAAN

vegetable fu yung

Beat the eggs with the salt and pepper. Heat the butter in a pan and pour in the eggs. Cook as an omelet, until set, remove from the pan, and cut into strips.

In a preheated wok or deep pan, heat the oil and stir-fry the garlic, until fragrant. Add the onion and stir-fry for 1 minute, then add the green bell pepper and stir for another minute. Stir in the rice and when the grains are separated, stir in the light soy sauce, and cook for 1 minute.

Add the scallion and egg strips, stir well, and finally add the bean sprouts and sesame oil. Stir-fry for 1 minute and serve.

COOK'S TIP
Use a nonstick wok or pan for this dish.

SERVES 4

4 tbsp vegetable oil or peanut oil

2 garlic cloves, finely chopped

2 fresh red chilies, seeded and chopped

1⅔ cups sliced mushrooms

¾ cup snow peas, halved

½ cup baby corn, halved

3 tbsp Thai soy sauce

1 tbsp jaggery or soft, light brown sugar

few fresh Thai basil leaves, plus extra sprigs to garnish

2 cups cooked rice, chilled

2 eggs, beaten

2 onions, sliced

KHAO-KHAI PAK HORM-TORD
egg-fried rice with vegetables and crispy onions

Heat half the oil in a wok or large skillet and cook the garlic and chilies for 2–3 minutes.

Add the mushrooms, snow peas, and corn and stir-fry for 2–3 minutes before adding the soy sauce, jaggery, and basil. Stir in the rice.

Push the mixture to one side of the wok and add the eggs to the bottom. Stir until lightly set before combining into the rice mixture.

Heat the remaining oil in another skillet and cook the onions, until crispy and brown. Serve the rice topped with the onions and garnished with basil sprigs.

COOK'S TIP
The rice must be cold when it is added to the wok, otherwise the egg will combine with it to make a congealed mass.

MAKES 4

4 small eggplants, about 5 inches/
　13 cm long

ghee, vegetable oil, or peanut oil,
　for cooking

STUFFING

4 firm tomatoes, grated

2 onions, grated

2 fresh red chilies, seeded or not,
　according to taste, and chopped

4 tbsp lemon juice

4 tbsp finely chopped fresh cilantro

1 tbsp Garlic and Ginger Paste

1½ tbsp ground coriander

2 tsp ground cumin

1 tsp fennel seeds

1 tsp ground turmeric

1 tsp salt

1 tbsp besan or gram flour (optional)

sprigs of fresh mint to garnish

Raita, to serve

150 BHARWAN BAINGAN TAMATTARI
tomato-stuffed eggplants

To make the stuffing, mix together the tomatoes, onions, chilies, lemon juice, fresh cilantro, garlic and ginger paste, ground coriander, ground cumin, fennel seeds, turmeric, and salt in a nonmetallic bowl. The filling should not be stiff, but thick enough so that it doesn't slide off the eggplant slices. If the tomatoes are very juicy and have made the filling too runny, gradually stir in about 1 tablespoon of besan flour.

To prepare the eggplants, work with one at a time. Slit each one into four parallel slices, from top to bottom, without cutting through the stem end, so that the eggplant remains in one piece. Lightly fan the slices apart, then use a small spoon or your fingers to fill, dividing one fourth of the stuffing between the slices and covering each slice to the edges. Carefully layer the slices back into position so that the eggplant looks whole again. Continue in the same way with the remaining eggplants. Choose a flameproof casserole or heavy-bottomed skillet with a tight-fitting lid that is large enough to hold the eggplants in a single layer. Melt enough ghee to cover the bottom of the pan with a layer about ¼ inch/5 mm deep, then add the eggplants in a single layer.

Put the pan over the lowest heat and cover tightly. Cook for 15 minutes, then carefully turn the eggplants over. Replace the lid on the pan and cook for another 10–15 minutes, or until the eggplants are tender when you pierce them with a skewer or a knife. Check occasionally while the eggplants are cooking, and if they start to stick to the bottom of the pan, stir in a couple of tablespoons of water. Serve hot or at room temperature with a Raita, garnished with mint.

SERVES 4

generous 1 cup yellow split lentils
  (channa dal), rinsed

5 cups water

1 tsp ground coriander

1 tsp ground cumin

¼ tsp ground asafetida

½ tsp ground turmeric

9 oz/250 g fresh spinach leaves, thick
  stems removed, sliced and rinsed

4 scallions, chopped

salt

TO GARNISH

3 tbsp vegetable oil or peanut oil

1 tsp mustard seeds

2 fresh green chilies, split lengthwise

½-inch/1-cm piece fresh gingerroot,
  very finely chopped

PALAK DAAL
spinach and lentils

Put the lentils and water in a large pan over high heat. Bring to a boil, reduce the heat to the lowest setting, and skim the surface as necessary.

When the foam stops rising, stir in the ground coriander, cumin, asafetida, and turmeric. Half-cover the pan and let the lentils simmer for 40 minutes, or until they are very tender and only a thin layer of liquid is left on top.

Stir the spinach and scallions into the lentils and continue simmering for another 5 minutes, stirring frequently, until the spinach is wilted. If the water evaporates before the spinach is cooked, stir in a little extra. Add salt to taste. Transfer the lentils to a serving dish.

To make the garnish, heat the oil in a small pan over high heat. Add the mustard seeds, chilies, and gingerroot and stir until the mustard seeds begin to pop and the chilies sizzle. Pour the oil and spices over the lentils to serve.

COOK'S TIP
The exact amount of water needed depends primarily on how old the lentils are, but also on the size of the pan. The older the lentils are, the longer simmering they will require to become tender. Unfortunately, there isn't any way to determine the age when you buy lentils, so be prepared to add extra water and increase the cooking time. Also, remember, the wider the pan, the quicker the water will evaporate.

SERVES 4

1 tbsp vegetable oil or peanut oil

1 tbsp chili oil

1 onion, chopped

2 garlic cloves, chopped

2 tbsp Thai red curry paste

1 small cauliflower, cut into florets

6 oz/175 g long green beans, cut into
    3-inch/7.5-cm lengths

⅔ cup vegetable bouillon

2 tbsp Thai soy sauce

scant ½ cup toasted cashews,
    to garnish

154 DAUNG-KA-LUM SAI TAU KHIAO, TAO OB

cauliflower and beans with cashews

Heat both the oils in a wok and stir-fry the onion and garlic until softened. Add the curry paste and stir-fry for 1–2 minutes.

Add the cauliflower and green beans and stir-fry for 3–4 minutes, or until softened. Pour in the bouillon and soy sauce and simmer for 1–2 minutes. Serve immediately, garnished with the cashews.

SERVES 4–6

generous 1 cup red split lentils
   (masoor dal), rinsed
6 oz/175 g new potatoes,
   scrubbed and finely diced
1 large carrot, finely diced
1 green bell pepper, cored,
   seeded, and finely chopped
4¼ cups water
¼ tsp ground turmeric
¼ tsp ground asafetida
1 tbsp tamarind paste
salt

SAMBHAR MASALA

3 dried red chilies,
   stems removed
2 tbsp coriander seeds
2 tsp cumin seeds
2 tsp black mustard seeds
1 tsp black peppercorns
1 tsp fenugreek seeds
3 cloves
¼ tsp ground turmeric
½ tsp ground asafetida
1½ tsp vegetable oil or
   peanut oil

1 tbsp dry unsweetened
   coconut
1½ tbsp yellow split lentils
   (channa dal)
1½ tbsp black split lentils
   (urad dal chilke)

TO GARNISH

1½ tbsp vegetable oil or
   peanut oil
12 fresh curry leaves or
   1 tbsp dried
2 dried red chilies
1 tsp black mustard seeds

SAMBHAR
sambhar

Put the red lentils in a bowl with enough water to cover and let soak for 30 minutes, changing the water once.

To make the Sambhar Masala, heat a skillet over medium-high heat. Add the chilies, coriander, cumin and mustard seeds, peppercorns, fenugreek seeds, and cloves. Dry-roast, stirring constantly, until the mustard seeds jump, you can smell the aromas and the seeds darken but do not burn. Add the turmeric and asafetida, then tip the spices into a bowl.

Return the pan to the heat. Add the oil and heat, then stir in the coconut and yellow and black lentils. Cook for 1 minute, until they darken. Tip out of the pan and add to the spices. Let cool, then place in a spice grinder or use a pestle and mortar to grind to a powder.

Drain the lentils. Put them in a large skillet with the potatoes, carrot, bell pepper, and water. Bring to a boil, skimming the surface as necessary. Reduce the heat to very low, stir in the turmeric and asafetida, and half-cover the pan. Simmer, stirring occasionally, for 15–20 minutes, or until the lentils are tender but not falling apart. Stir in the tamarind paste and 2 teaspoons of the Sambhar Masala. Taste and add extra masala and salt to taste.

Meanwhile, to make the garnish, heat the oil in a large pan over high heat. Add the curry leaves, chilies, and mustard seeds and stir quickly. Transfer the lentils to a serving dish and pour the hot oil and spices over.

COOK'S TIP
Store any leftover masala in a sealed jar in the refrigerator for up to 4 months.

MAKES 16

2 tbsp vegetable oil or peanut oil

8 oz/225 g potatoes, diced and boiled
  for 5 minutes

2 garlic cloves, crushed

1 onion, chopped

2 tbsp Thai green curry paste

2 oz/55 g frozen peas, thawed

juice of 1 lime

½ tsp salt

16 spring roll wrappers, about
  4 inches/10 cm square

1 egg, beaten

vegetable oil or peanut oil, for
  deep-frying

sweet chili sauce or Thai soy sauce,
  to serve

PUK HAO

vegetable packets

Heat the oil in a wok or skillet and stir-fry the potatoes, garlic, onion, and curry paste until lightly browned. Stir in the peas, lime juice, and salt and stir-fry for 1–2 minutes. Remove from the heat.

Brush 1 spring roll wrapper with egg. Put a small spoonful of the potato mixture in the middle and fold up the edges to enclose the filling and make a purse-shaped packet. Press the wrapper tightly together to seal the packet. Repeat with the remaining wrappers and filling to make 16 small packets.

Heat enough oil for deep-frying in a wok, deep-fat fryer, or large, heavy-bottomed pan, until it reaches 350–375°F/180–190°C, or until a cube of bread browns in 30 seconds. Add the vegetable packets, in batches, and deep-fry for 3–4 minutes, or until golden brown. Drain on paper towels and keep warm while you cook the remaining packets. Serve hot with a bowl of chili sauce or soy sauce for dipping.

SERVES 4–6

generous 1 cup whole black lentils
  (urad dal sabat)

⅔ cup dried red kidney beans

4 garlic cloves, cut in half

4 black cardamom pods, lightly crushed

2 bay leaves

1 cinnamon stick

½ cup unsalted butter

1½ tbsp Garlic and Ginger Paste

2 tbsp tomato paste

½ tsp chili powder

pinch of sugar

salt

⅔ cup heavy cream

few sprigs of fresh cilantro, to garnish

MAAH KI DAAL
black dal

Put the lentils and kidney beans in separate bowls with plenty of water to cover and let soak for at least 3 hours, but ideally overnight.

Meanwhile, put the garlic cloves, cardamom pods, bay leaves, and cinnamon stick in a piece of cheesecloth and tie together into a bundle.

Drain the lentils and kidney beans separately. Put the beans in a pan with twice their volume of water and bring to a boil. Boil for 10 minutes, then drain. Return the beans to the pan, add the lentils, and cover with double their volume of water. Add the spice bag and bring to a boil, then reduce the heat to low and simmer, partially covered, for 3 hours, skimming the surface as necessary, until the beans are reduced to a thick paste. Mash the beans against the side of the pan with a wooden spoon every 15 minutes while simmering.

When the beans are almost ready, remove the spice bag and set aside to cool. Melt the butter in a pan. Add the garlic and ginger paste and stir for 1 minute. Stir in the tomato paste, chili powder, and sugar, and salt to taste; simmer for 2–3 minutes. When the spice bag is cool enough to handle, squeeze the juices into the beans. Stir the butter and spice mixture into the beans, along with all but 2 tablespoons of the cream. Bring to a boil, then lower the heat and simmer for 10 minutes, stirring occasionally. Transfer the dal to a serving dish, swirl with the remaining cream, and garnish with the cilantro sprigs.

COOK'S TIP
While the beans are simmering, add more water if the liquid evaporates before they are tender.

SERVES 4

2 tbsp vegetable oil or peanut oil

2 red onions, sliced

2 garlic cloves, finely chopped

2-inch/5-cm piece fresh gingerroot, finely chopped

1 red chili, seeded and chopped

1 tbsp Thai Red Curry Paste

8 oz/225 g potatoes, cut into cubes, boiled for 5 minutes, and drained

2 red bell peppers, cored, seeded, and diced

1¼ cups vegetable bouillon

1 tsp salt

4 tbsp chopped fresh cilantro

KAENG PED MUN FA RUNG SAI HOM YAI, PHRIK YHUAK

onion, potato, and red bell pepper curry

Heat the oil in a wok or large skillet and stir-fry the onions, garlic, gingerroot, and chili for 2–3 minutes. Add the curry paste and stir-fry over low heat for 2–3 minutes.

Add the potatoes, bell peppers, bouillon, and salt and cook for 3–4 minutes, or until all the vegetables are tender. Stir in the cilantro and serve immediately.

SERVES 4–6

2 tbsp vegetable oil or peanut oil

1 tsp mustard seeds

7 oz/200 g shallots, thinly sliced

1 tbsp Garlic and Ginger Paste

12 fresh curry leaves or 1 tbsp dried

2 dried red chilies

2 fresh green chilies, seeded or not,
  according to taste, and chopped

½ tsp ground coriander

½ tsp ground turmeric

8 large, firm ripe tomatoes, about
  1 lb 5 oz/600 g, chopped

1½ tbsp tomato paste

1¼ cups plain yogurt

sprigs of fresh mint, chopped
  and whole to garnish

salt

TAMATTAR KA RAITA
hot tomato raita

Heat the oil in a wok or large skillet over medium-high heat. Add the mustard seeds and stir them around until they start to jump and crackle.

Stir in the shallots, and garlic and ginger paste and stir for 5 minutes, or until the shallots are golden.

Add the curry leaves, dried chilies, green chilies, coriander, and turmeric, lower the heat, and stir for 30 seconds.

Add the tomatoes and tomato paste to the pan and simmer for 5 minutes, stirring gently, to soften and heat the tomatoes, but not to break them up completely.

Remove the pan from the heat and gradually stir in the yogurt, beating well after each addition. Add the chopped mint. Taste and add salt if necessary. Cover the pan and let stand for 2–3 minutes, then stir gently. Serve garnished with the chopped and whole sprigs of fresh mint.

COOK'S TIP
Plain yogurt varies in its sourness, depending on the brand. If you find this dish too sour, stir in jaggery or light brown sugar.

SERVES 4

2 tbsp vegetable oil or peanut oil, plus extra for deep-frying

8 oz/225 g firm bean curd (drained weight), drained and cut into cubes

1 tbsp chili oil

2 fresh green chilies, seeded and sliced

2 garlic cloves, crushed

6 scallions, sliced

2 zucchini, cut into batons

½ cucumber, peeled, seeded, and sliced

1 green bell pepper, cored, seeded, and sliced

1 small head broccoli, cut into florets

2 oz/55 g fine green beans, halved

½ cup frozen peas, thawed

1¼ cups vegetable bouillon

4 tbsp coconut cream

2 tbsp Thai soy sauce

1 tsp jaggery or soft, light brown sugar

4 tbsp chopped fresh parsley, to garnish (optional)

KAENG KHIAO WAN TAO HU

bean curd and green vegetable curry

Heat the oil for deep-frying in a skillet and carefully lower in the bean curd cubes, in batches, and cook for 2–3 minutes, or until golden brown. Remove with a slotted spoon and drain on paper towels.

Heat 2 tablespoons of the vegetable oil and all the chili oil in a wok and stir-fry the chilies, garlic, and scallions for 2–3 minutes. Add the zucchini, cucumber, green bell pepper, broccoli, and green beans and stir-fry for another 2–3 minutes.

Add the peas, bouillon, coconut, soy sauce, and jaggery. Cover and simmer for 2–3 minutes, or until all the vegetables are tender.

Stir in the bean curd and serve immediately, sprinkled with the parsley, if using.

SERVES 4–6

½ fresh coconut, containing about
    4½ oz/125 g of coconut flesh

1 fresh green chili, seeded and chopped

1½ tsp sugar

1 tsp ground coriander

¾ tsp ground cumin

¼ tsp chili powder

2 bay leaves

2 tbsp ghee, vegetable oil, or peanut oil

1 lb 5 oz/600 g pumpkin, peeled, seeded,
    and coarsely grated

1 tsp garam masala

KADDU AUR NARIYAL KI SABZI

spiced pumpkin and coconut

If you are using a whole coconut, use a hammer and nail to punch a hole in the "eye" of the coconut, then pour out, and reserve the liquid from the inside.

Measure the coconut liquid and add water, if necessary, to make a generous 1 cup. Add the chili, sugar, coriander, cumin, chili powder, and bay leaves to the coconut liquid, and set aside.

Use the hammer to break the coconut in half, then peel half, and grate the flesh on the coarse side of a grater, or whizz in a food processor (save the other half to use in another recipe).

Melt the ghee in a wok or large skillet over medium heat. Add the pumpkin and stir for 1 minute. Add the grated coconut and continue stirring, until the mixture starts to turn brown.

Stir in the coconut water. Increase the heat and continue stir-frying, until only about 4 tablespoons of liquid are left. Sprinkle with the garam masala and continue stir-frying, until all the liquid has evaporated. Serve immediately.

COOK'S TIP
Before you buy a coconut, shake it. If you hear a lot of liquid slushing around inside, it is fresh. If you can't find a fresh coconut, use 1½ cups dry unsweetened coconut and stir-fry the pumpkin and coconut in a generous 1 cup coconut milk.

SERVES 4

2 tbsp vegetable oil or peanut oil

1 fresh green chili, seeded and chopped

6 scallions, sliced

3 tbsp Thai green curry paste

4 oz/115 g bok choy

4 oz/115 g napa cabbage

4 oz/115 g spinach

4 oz/115 g asparagus

3 celery stalks, diagonally sliced

3 tbsp Thai soy sauce

1 tsp jaggery or soft, light
  brown sugar

juice of 1 lime

boiled jasmine rice, to serve

KAENG KHIAO WAN RUAM
mixed greens curry

Heat the oil in a wok or large skillet and stir-fry the chili and scallions for 1–2 minutes. Add the curry paste and stir-fry for 2–3 minutes.

Add the bok choy, napa cabbage, spinach, asparagus, and celery and stir-fry for 3–4 minutes, or until just tender.

Add the soy sauce, jaggery, and lime juice and cook for 30 seconds to heat through. Serve immediately with jasmine rice.

SERVES 4–6

3 oz/85 g cashews

1½ tbsp Garlic and Ginger Paste

generous ¾ cup water

4 tbsp ghee, vegetable oil, or peanut oil

1 large onion, chopped

5 green cardamom pods, lightly crushed

1 cinnamon stick, broken in half

¼ tsp ground turmeric

generous 1 cup heavy cream

5 oz/140 g new potatoes, scrubbed and
   chopped into ½-inch/1-cm pieces

5 oz/140 g cauliflower florets

½ tsp garam masala

5 oz/140 g eggplant, chopped into
   chunks

5 oz/140 g green beans, chopped
   into ½-inch/1-cm pieces

salt and pepper

fresh mint or cilantro, chopped,
   to garnish

SABZI KA KORMA
cauliflower, eggplant, and green bean korma

Heat a large, flameproof casserole or skillet with a tight-fitting lid over high heat. Add the cashews and stir until they start to brown, then tip them out of the casserole.

Put the nuts in a spice blender with the garlic and ginger paste and 1 tablespoon of the water, and whizz until a coarse paste forms.

Melt the ghee in the casserole over medium-high heat. Add the onion and cook for 5–8 minutes, or until golden brown. Add the nut paste and stir for 5 minutes. Stir in the cardamom pods, cinnamon stick, and turmeric. Add the cream and the remaining water and bring to a boil, stirring. Reduce the heat to the lowest level, cover the casserole, and simmer for 5 minutes.

Add the potatoes, cauliflower, and garam masala and simmer, covered, for 5 minutes. Stir in the eggplant and green beans and continue simmering for another 5 minutes, or until all the vegetables are tender. Check the sauce occasionally to make sure it isn't sticking on the bottom of the pan, and stir in extra water if needed.

Taste and add seasoning, if necessary. Sprinkle with the mint or cilantro to serve.

COOK'S TIP
When you serve this, remember to tell guests that it contains cardamom pods, which taste bitter if you bite into them.

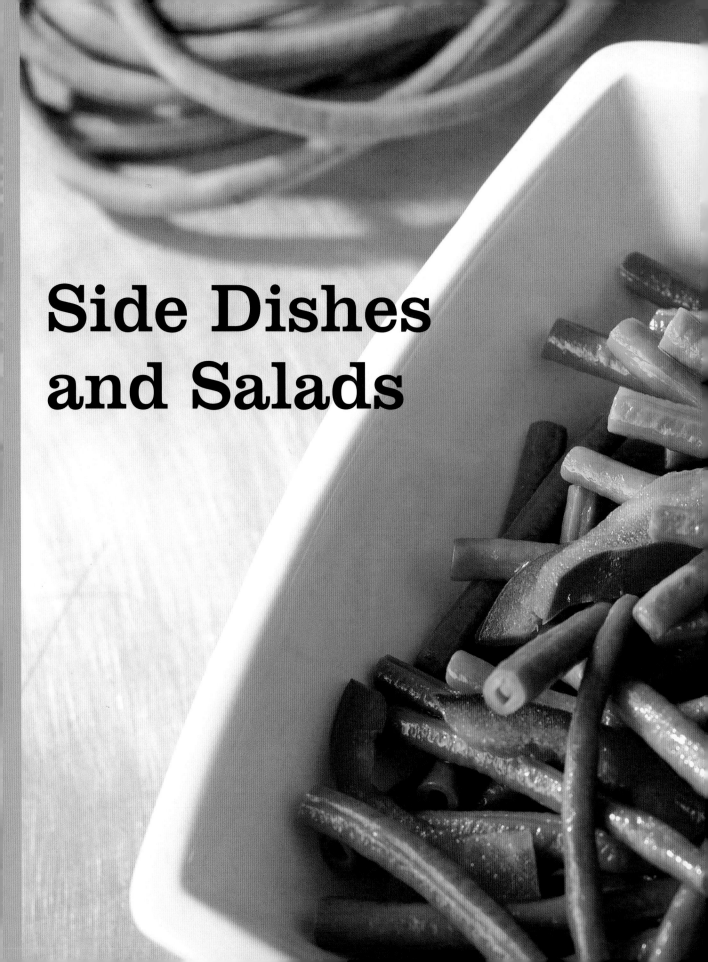

Side Dishes and Salads

SERVES 3–4
generous 1 cup long-grain rice

SI MIU BAAK FAAN
steamed white rice

Wash and drain the rice. Place in a pan with the same volume of water plus a little extra
(the water should just cover the rice). Bring to a boil, cover, and simmer for about 15 minutes.
Turn off the heat and let the rice continue to cook in its own steam for about 5 minutes.
At this point, the grains should be cooked through but not sticking together.

COOK'S TIP
This recipe is for a standard long-grain rice, such as jasmine rice. Allow a little more water
and a little more time for basmati.

SERVES 4–6

generous 1 cup basmati rice

2 tbsp ghee, vegetable oil, or peanut oil

1 tsp nigella seeds

scant 2 cups water

juice and finely grated zest
 of 1 large lemon

1½ tsp salt

¼ tsp ground turmeric

NIMBU BHAAT
lemon rice

Rinse the basmati rice in several changes of water until the water runs clear, then let soak for 30 minutes. Drain and set aside until ready to cook.

Melt the ghee in a flameproof casserole or large pan with a tight-fitting lid over medium-high heat. Add the nigella seeds and the rice and stir until all the grains are coated in ghee. Add the water and bring to a boil.

Reduce the heat to as low as possible, stir in half the lemon juice, the salt, and turmeric, and cover the casserole tightly. Simmer, without lifting the lid, for 8–10 minutes, or until the grains are tender and all the liquid is absorbed.

Turn off the heat and use 2 forks to mix the remaining juice into the rice. Adjust the seasoning, if necessary. Replace the lid on the casserole and let the rice stand for 5 minutes. Garnish with lemon zest and serve.

VARIATION

To make Lemon and Cashew Rice, melt the ghee, then add ½ cup cashews, and stir them around for 30 seconds, or until golden. Use a slotted spoon to remove them from the casserole immediately so they do not become too brown. Add 1 teaspoon fenugreek seeds with the nigella seeds and continue with the recipe. Stir the cashews into the rice with the lemon zest and juice, then replace the lid on the pan and let stand for 5 minutes. Serve garnished with chopped fresh mint.

SERVES 4

2 tbsp vegetable oil or peanut oil

2 cups cooked rice, chilled

1 egg, well beaten

DAAN FA CHAAU FAAN
egg-fried rice

Heat the oil in a preheated wok or deep pan and stir-fry the rice for 1 minute, breaking it down as much as possible into individual grains.

Quickly add the egg, stirring, so as to coat each piece of rice. Stir until the egg is cooked and the rice, as far as possible, is in single grains. Serve the rice immediately.

COOK'S TIP
Break up the rice as much as possible after chilling it to make the dish easier to cook.

SERVES 4

3 tbsp ghee, vegetable oil, or peanut oil

1 onion, thinly sliced

1 lb 2 oz/500 g okra, stem ends
trimmed off

1 or 2 fresh green chilies, seeded
or not, according to taste, and sliced

2 tsp ground cumin

¼ tsp garam masala

salt and pepper

lemon wedges, to serve

BHINDI KI SABZI
spiced okra

Melt the ghee in a wok or large skillet over medium-high heat. Add the onion and cook, stirring frequently, for 2 minutes.

Add the okra, green chilies, and cumin, and salt and pepper to taste and continue cooking, stirring, for 5 minutes.

Sprinkle with the garam masala and continue stirring for another 2 minutes, or until the okra are tender but still crisp. Serve with lemon wedges for squeezing over.

VARIATION
Add 2 seeded and chopped tomatoes with the okra and chilies, or remove the pan from the heat when the okra is tender and slowly stir in generous 1 cup plain yogurt, a little at a time, beating constantly.

SERVES 4–6

10 oz/280 g long green beans, cut into
   2½-inch/6-cm lengths

1 tbsp vegetable oil or peanut oil

1 red bell pepper, cored, seeded,
   and cut into strips

pinch of salt

pinch of sugar

DANG LUNG JIU CHAAU DAU GO
stir-fried green beans with red bell pepper

Blanch the beans in a large pan of boiling water for 30 seconds. Drain and set aside.

In a preheated wok or deep pan, heat the oil and stir-fry the beans for 1 minute over high heat. Add the bell pepper and stir-fry for 1 minute. Sprinkle the salt and sugar on top and serve.

COOK'S TIP
In China, long green beans are traditionally cooked with egg or black beans or, as in this recipe, a second vegetable that supplies a beautiful color contrast.

SERVES 4–6

4 tbsp ghee, vegetable oil, or peanut oil

½ tbsp cumin seeds

1 onion, chopped

1½-inch/4-cm piece fresh gingerroot, finely chopped

1 fresh green chili, seeded and thinly sliced

1 lb/450 g cauliflower, cut into small florets

1 lb/450 g large waxy potatoes, peeled and cut into large chunks

½ tsp ground coriander

½ tsp garam masala

salt

few sprigs of fresh cilantro, to garnish

aloo gobi

Melt the ghee in a flameproof casserole or large skillet with a tight-fitting lid over medium-high heat. Add the cumin seeds and stir around for 30 seconds, or until they crackle and start to brown.

Immediately stir in the onion, gingerroot, and chili and stir for 5–8 minutes, or until the onion is golden.

Stir in the cauliflower and potatoes, followed by the ground coriander, garam masala, and salt to taste, and continue stirring for about 30 seconds longer.

Cover the pan, reduce the heat to the lowest setting, and simmer, stirring occasionally, for 20–30 minutes, or until the vegetables are tender when pierced with the point of a knife. Check occasionally that they aren't sticking to the bottom of the pan and stir in a little water, if necessary.

Taste and adjust the seasoning, if necessary, and sprinkle with the cilantro to serve.

VARIATION
For a more golden-colored dish, add ¼ teaspoon ground turmeric with the other ground spices.

MAKES ABOUT 8 DOSAS

generous ½ cup basmati rice, rinsed
   and drained

⅓ cup split black lentils
   (urad dal chilke)

¼ tsp fenugreek seeds

½ cup water

2 tbsp ghee, melted, or 2 tbsp vegetable
   oil or peanut oil

salt

dosas

Bring a pan of salted water to a boil, add the basmati rice, and boil for 5 minutes, then drain. Put the rice, split black lentils, and fenugreek seeds in a bowl, cover with water, and let soak overnight.

The next day, strain the rice and lentils, reserving the soaking liquid. Put the rice and lentils in a food processor with 5 tablespoons of the water, and whizz until a smooth, sludgy, gray paste forms. Slowly add the remaining water. Cover the bowl with a dish towel that has been soaked in hot water and wrung out, and let ferment in a warm place for 5–6 hours, until small bubbles appear all over the surface.

Stir the mixture and add as much extra water as necessary to get a consistency of light cream. Add salt to taste. The amount of salt you need depends on how "sour" tasting the batter is.

Heat the flattest, largest pan you have over high heat, until a splash of water "dances" when it hits the surface, then brush the surface with melted ghee. Put a ladleful of batter in the center of the pan and use the bottom of the ladle to spread it out as thinly as possible in concentric circles, then let it cook for 2 minutes, until it is golden brown and crisp on the bottom.

Flip the dosa over using a metal spatula and continue cooking for another 2 minutes. Turn out of the pan and keep warm if you are going to wrap around a filling or let it cool. Continue until all the batter has been used.

MAKES 12

generous 1½ cups whole-wheat flour, sifted, plus extra for dusting

½ tbsp salt

2 tbsp ghee, melted, or 2 tbsp vegetable oil or peanut oil

⅓–⅔ cup water

vegetable oil or peanut oil, for deep-frying

PURIS
pooris

Put the flour and salt into a bowl and drizzle the ghee over the surface. Gradually stir in the water until a stiff dough forms.

Turn out the dough onto a lightly floured counter and knead for 10 minutes, or until it is smooth and elastic. Shape the dough into a ball and place it in the cleaned bowl, then cover with a damp dish towel and let rest for 20 minutes.

Divide the dough into 12 equal pieces and roll each into a ball. Working with one ball of dough at a time, flatten the dough between your palms, then roll it out thinly on a lightly floured counter into a 5-inch/13-cm circle. Continue until all the dough balls are rolled out.

Heat at least 3 inches/7.5 cm oil in a wok, deep-fat fryer, or large skillet, until it reaches 350–375°F/180–190°C, or until a cube of bread browns in 30 seconds. Drop one poori into the hot fat and deep-fry for 10 seconds, or until it puffs up. Use 2 large spoons to flip the poori over and spoon some hot oil over the top.

Use the 2 spoons to lift the poori from the oil, and let any excess oil drip back into the pan. Drain the poori on crumpled paper towels and serve immediately. Continue until all the pooris are cooked, making sure the oil returns to the correct temperature before you add another poori.

MAKES 10

7 cups strong white flour

1 tbsp baking powder

1 tsp sugar

1 tsp salt

1¼ cups water, heated to 122°F/50°C

1 egg, beaten

4 tbsp ghee, melted, or 4 tbsp vegetable
   oil or peanut oil, plus a little extra for
   rolling out and brushing

NAANS
nans

Sift the flour, baking powder, sugar, and salt into a mixing bowl and make a well in the center. Mix together the water and egg until blended. Slowly pour the liquid mixture into the well, using your fingers to draw in the flour from the sides, until a heavy dough forms. Shape the dough into a ball and return to the bowl. Soak a clean dish towel in hot water, then wring it out and use it to cover the bowl, tucking the ends under the bowl. Let the dough rest for 30 minutes.

Turn out the dough onto a counter brushed with melted ghee. Flatten the dough, then sprinkle with the melted ghee and knead to work it in. Shape the dough into 10 equal balls. Resoak the towel in hot water and wring it out again, then place it over the dough balls and let them rest and rise for 1 hour.

Meanwhile, put 2 cookie sheets in the oven and preheat it to 450°F/230°C.

Use a lightly greased rolling pin to roll the dough balls into teardrop shapes, about ⅛ inch/ 3 mm thick. Use crumpled paper towels to rub the hot cookie sheets with ghee. Arrange the nans on the sheets and bake for 5–6 minutes, or until golden brown and puffed. As you take the nans out of the oven, brush with melted ghee and serve immediately.

VARIATIONS
To make Garlic and Nigella Seed Nans, just before baking scatter the dough with 3 thinly sliced garlic cloves and 2 tablespoons of nigella seeds. For Sesame Nans, sprinkle the dough with 2 tablespoons of sesame seeds just before it is baked.

MAKES 8

generous 1½ cups whole-wheat flour,
  sifted, plus extra for dusting

½ tsp salt

⅔ cup–generous ¾ cup water

⅔ cup ghee, melted, or ⅔ cup vegetable
  oil or peanut oil

parathas

Mix the flour and salt together in a bowl and make a well in the center. Gradually stir in enough water to make a stiff dough. Turn out the dough onto a lightly floured counter and knead for 10 minutes, or until smooth and elastic. Shape the dough into a ball and place it in the cleaned bowl; cover with a damp dish towel and let rest for 20 minutes.

Divide the dough into 8 equal pieces. Lightly flour your hands and roll each piece of dough into a ball. Working with one ball at a time, roll it out on a lightly floured counter to make a 5-inch/13-cm circle. Brush the top with about 1½ teaspoons of the melted ghee. Fold the circle in half to make a half-moon shape and brush the top again with melted ghee. Fold in half again to make a triangle. Press the layers together.

Roll out the triangle on a lightly floured counter into a larger triangle that is about 7 inches/ 18 cm on each side. Flip the dough back and forth between your hands a couple of times, then cover with a damp cloth and continue, until all the dough is shaped and rolled.

Meanwhile, heat an ungreased skillet or stove top grill pan over high heat until very hot and a splash of water "dances" when it hits the surface. Place a paratha in the pan and cook until bubbles appear on the surface. Use tongs to flip the paratha over and brush the surface with melted ghee. Continue cooking until the bottom is golden brown, then flip the paratha over again and smear with more melted ghee. Use a wooden spoon or spatula to press down on the surface of the paratha so it cooks evenly.

Brush with melted ghee and serve; repeat with the remaining parathas. These are best served immediately, but can be kept warm wrapped in foil for about 20 minutes.

MAKES 6

generous 1½ cups whole-wheat flour, sifted, plus extra for dusting

½ tsp salt

⅔ cup–generous ¾ cup water

melted ghee, or vegetable oil or peanut oil, for brushing

chapatis

Mix the flour and salt together in a bowl and make a well in the center. Gradually stir in enough water to make a stiff dough. Turn out the dough onto a lightly floured counter and knead for 10 minutes, or until smooth and elastic. Shape the dough into a ball and place it in the cleaned bowl, then cover with a damp dish towel, and let rest for 20 minutes.

Divide the dough into 6 equal pieces. Lightly flour your hands and roll each piece of dough into a ball. Meanwhile, heat a large, ungreased skillet or stove top grill pan over high heat, until very hot and a splash of water "dances" when it hits the surface.

Working with 1 ball at a time, flatten the dough between your palms, then roll it out on a lightly floured counter into a 7-inch/18-cm round. Slap the dough onto the hot pan and cook until brown flecks appear on the bottom. Flip over using tongs or a metal spatula and repeat on the other side.

Flip the dough over again and use a bunched-up dish towel to press down all around the edge. This pushes the steam in the chapati around, causing the chapati to puff up. Cook until the bottom is golden brown, then flip over and repeat this step on the other side.

Brush the chapati with melted ghee and serve, then repeat with the remaining dough balls. Chapatis are best served immediately, as soon as they come out of the pan, but they can be kept warm wrapped in foil for about 20 minutes.

MAKES ABOUT 9 oz/250 g

1 large mango, about 14 oz/400 g,
  peeled, pitted, and finely chopped

2 tbsp lime juice

1 tbsp vegetable oil or peanut oil

2 shallots, finely chopped

1 garlic clove, finely chopped

2 fresh green chilies, seeded and
  thinly sliced

1 tsp black mustard seeds

1 tsp coriander seeds

5 tbsp grated jaggery or light
  brown sugar

5 tbsp white wine vinegar

1 tsp salt

pinch of ground ginger

AAM KI CHUTNEY
mango chutney

Put the mango in a nonmetallic bowl with the lime juice and set aside.

Heat the oil in a large skillet or pan over medium-high heat. Add the shallots and cook for 3 minutes. Add the garlic and chilies and stir for another 2 minutes, or until the shallots are soft but not brown. Add the mustard and coriander seeds and then stir.

Add the mango to the pan with the jaggery, vinegar, salt, and ground ginger and stir. Reduce the heat to its lowest setting and simmer for 10 minutes, or until the liquid thickens and the mango becomes sticky.

Remove from the heat and let cool completely. Transfer to an airtight container, cover, and chill for 3 days before using. Store in the refrigerator and use within 1 week.

MAKES ABOUT 8 oz/225 g

1½ tbsp lemon juice

1½ tbsp water

1½ cups fresh cilantro leaves and stems, coarsely chopped

2 tbsp chopped fresh coconut

1 small shallot, very finely chopped

¼-inch/5-mm piece fresh gingerroot, chopped

1 fresh green chili, seeded and chopped

½ tsp sugar

½ tsp salt

pinch of pepper

HARE DHANIYE KI CHUTNEY
cilantro chutney

Put the lemon juice and water in a small food processor, add half the cilantro, and whizz until it is blended and a slushy paste forms. Gradually add the remaining cilantro and whizz until it is all blended, scraping down the sides of the processor, if necessary.

If you don't have a processor that will cope with this small amount, use a pestle and mortar, adding the cilantro in small amounts.

Add the remaining ingredients and continue whizzing, until they are all finely chopped and blended. Taste and adjust any of the seasonings, if desired. Transfer to a nonmetallic bowl, cover with plastic wrap, and chill for up to 3 days before serving.

VARIATION
To make a cooling Cilantro Raita, stir 1¼ cups plain yogurt into the chutney and chill for at least 1 hour. Sprinkle with plenty of chopped fresh cilantro just before serving.

SERVES 4–6

1 large piece of cucumber, about
  10½ oz/300 g, rinsed

1 tsp salt

1¾ cups plain yogurt

½ tsp sugar

pinch of ground cumin

2 tbsp chopped fresh cilantro or mint

chili powder, to garnish

raita

Lay a clean dish towel flat on a counter. Coarsely grate the unpeeled cucumber directly onto the towel. Sprinkle with ½ teaspoon of the salt, then gather up the towel and squeeze, until all the excess moisture is removed from the cucumber.

Put the yogurt into a bowl and beat in the remaining ½ teaspoon of salt, along with the sugar and cumin. Stir in the grated cucumber. Taste and add extra seasoning, if desired. Cover with plastic wrap and chill.

Stir in the chopped cilantro and transfer to a serving bowl. Sprinkle with chili powder and serve.

VARIATIONS
Stir in 2 seeded and finely chopped tomatoes or 4 finely chopped scallions, with the cilantro or mint. Ground coriander or ginger can also be added to taste. To make a Banana Raita, peel and slice 3 bananas directly into the yogurt, then stir in 2 seeded and chopped fresh green chilies and 1 tablespoon of garam masala. Add a little lemon zest and juice, if desired. Cover with plastic wrap and chill until required, then stir in the chopped fresh cilantro or mint just before serving.

SERVES 4

4 tbsp vegetable oil or peanut oil

bunch of scallions, chopped

6 oz/175 g Chinese or purple
  sprouting broccoli

½ small cabbage (any variety), shredded

8 oz/225 g fresh spinach, washed

8 oz/225 g bok choy, halved or cut into
  fourths if necessary

1 small head napa cabbage, shredded

few sprigs of fresh Thai basil

2 fresh red chilies, seeded and chopped

2 tbsp oyster sauce

1 tsp jaggery or soft, light
  brown sugar

1 tbsp sesame oil

2 tbsp sesame seeds, toasted

PAHD PUK

stir-fried vegetable salad

Heat 2 tablespoons of oil in a wok or large skillet and cook the scallions, broccoli, all the greens, the basil, and the chilies quickly, until just wilted. Transfer to a serving plate.

Mix the oyster sauce, sugar, the remaining vegetable oil, and the sesame oil together and pour over the greens.

Scatter the sesame seeds over the top and serve immediately.

SERVES 4–6

1 lb/450 g carrots, peeled

1 tbsp vegetable oil or peanut oil

½ tbsp black mustard seeds

½ tbsp cumin seeds

1 fresh green chili, seeded and chopped

½ tsp sugar

½ tsp salt

pinch of ground turmeric

1½–2 tbsp lemon juice

GAJAR NU SALAT
gujarat carrot salad

Grate the carrots on the coarse side of a grater into a bowl, then set aside.

Heat the oil in a wok or large skillet over medium-high heat. Add the mustard and cumin seeds and cook, stirring, until the mustard seeds start popping. Immediately remove the pan from the heat and stir in the chili, sugar, salt, and turmeric. Let the spices cool for about 5 minutes.

Pour the warm spices and any oil over the carrots, then add the lemon juice. Toss together and adjust the seasoning, if necessary, then cover with plastic wrap and chill for at least 30 minutes. Give the salad a good toss just before serving.

SERVES 4–6

2 large tomatoes

DRESSING

1 tbsp finely chopped scallion

1 tsp finely chopped garlic

½ tsp sesame oil

1 tbsp white rice vinegar

½ tsp salt

pinch of white pepper

pinch of sugar

CHUNG SIK FAAN KE SA LEUT
chinese tomato salad

Mix together all the ingredients for the dressing and set aside.

Thinly slice the tomatoes. Arrange on a plate and spoon the dressing over the top.

COOK'S TIP

Use ripe but firm tomatoes and slice very thinly with a very sharp knife.

SERVES 4

2 tbsp vegetable oil or peanut oil

1 tbsp chili oil

1 onion, sliced

1-inch/2.5-cm piece gingerroot, grated

1 small head broccoli, cut into florets

2 carrots, cut into batons

1 red bell pepper, cored, seeded, and cut into squares

1 yellow bell pepper, cored, seeded, and cut into strips

¾ cup snow peas, trimmed and halved

½ cup baby corn, halved

DRESSING

2 tbsp vegetable oil or peanut oil

1 tsp chili oil

1 tbsp rice wine vinegar

juice of 1 lime

½ tsp Thai fish sauce

YUM PUK
hot-and-sour vegetable salad

Heat the oils in a wok or large skillet and cook the onion and ginger for 1–2 minutes, or until they start to soften. Add the vegetables and stir-fry for 2–3 minutes, or until they have softened slightly. Remove from the heat and set aside.

Mix the dressing ingredients together. Transfer the vegetables to a serving plate and drizzle the dressing over. Serve warm immediately, or let the flavors develop and serve cold.

SERVES 4

1 papaya, peeled

12 oz/350 g large cooked peeled shrimp

assorted baby salad greens, to serve

DRESSING

4 scallions, finely chopped

2 fresh red chilies, seeded and
  finely chopped

1 tsp Thai fish sauce

1 tbsp vegetable oil or peanut oil

juice of 1 lime

1 tsp jaggery or soft, light
  brown sugar

212 SOMTAM GUNG
shrimp and papaya salad

Scoop the seeds out of the papaya and slice the flesh thinly. Stir gently together with the shrimp.

Mix the dressing ingredients together in a separate bowl.

Arrange the salad greens in a bowl and top with the papaya and shrimp. Pour the dressing over and serve immediately.

Desserts

SERVES 6

4 apples, peeled, cored, and each
  cut into 8 rings, lengthwise
vegetable oil or peanut oil, for
  deep-frying

BATTER

generous ¾ cup all-purpose flour
1 egg, beaten
½ cup cold water

TOFFEE SYRUP

4 tbsp sesame oil
generous 1 cup sugar
2 tbsp sesame seeds, toasted

216 BAT SI PING GWO
toffee apple slices

To prepare the batter, sift the flour and stir in the egg. Slowly add the water, beating to achieve a smooth and thick batter. Dip each apple ring in the batter.

Heat enough oil for deep-frying in a wok, deep-fat fryer, or large heavy-bottomed pan, until it reaches 350–375°F/180–190°C, or until a cube of bread browns in 30 seconds. Deep-fry the apple rings, until golden brown. Drain and set aside.

To make the Toffee Syrup, heat the sesame oil in a small, heavy-bottomed pan and, when beginning to smoke, add the sugar, stirring constantly, until the mixture caramelizes and turns golden. Remove from the heat, stir in the sesame seeds, and pour into a large, flat pan.

Over very low heat, place the apple slices in the syrup, turning once. When coated, dip each slice in cold water. Serve immediately.

COOK'S TIP
Work quickly to insure the syrup does not set and in order to seal the syrup on each apple ring.

SERVES 4

1 pineapple

1 mango, peeled, pitted, and sliced

4 tbsp unsalted butter

4 tbsp light corn syrup

1–2 tsp ground cinnamon

1 tsp freshly grated nutmeg

4 tbsp soft brown sugar

2 passion fruit

⅔ cup sour cream

finely grated zest of 1 orange

SUBPAROT OB
roasted spicy pineapple

Preheat the oven to 400°F/200°C. Use a sharp knife to cut off the top, bottom, and skin of the pineapple, then cut into fourths. Remove the central core and cut the flesh into large cubes. Place them in a roasting pan with the mango.

Place the butter, syrup, cinnamon, nutmeg, and sugar in a small pan and heat gently, stirring constantly, until melted. Pour the mixture over the fruit. Roast for 20–30 minutes, or until the fruit is browned.

Halve the passion fruit and scoop out the seeds. Spoon over the roasted fruit. Mix the sour cream and orange zest together and serve with the fruit.

SERVES 4–6

vegetable oil or peanut oil, for cooking

4–5 medium-ripe bananas, halved and
  cut into 2¾-inch/7-cm long chunks

BATTER

generous ⅓ cup all-purpose flour

pinch of salt

1 egg, beaten

generous 3 tbsp milk

scant 2 tbsp sugar

JA HEUNG JIU
banana fritters

To prepare the batter, sift the flour and salt into a bowl. Stir in the beaten egg, then gradually add the milk, beating to create a smooth, thick batter. Stir in the sugar.

Heat some oil in a wok or deep skillet. Dip each banana piece into the batter and cook for about 3–4 minutes, or until golden brown. Drain and serve warm.

COOK'S TIP
Add a little butter to the oil for an even more delicious result, or use only butter for cooking, taking care not to burn it.

SERVES 4

4 tbsp coconut cream

⅔ cup heavy cream

4 bananas

juice and zest of 1 lime

1 tbsp vegetable oil or peanut oil

generous ½ cup dry unsweetened
  coconut

KHUAY PING
griddled bananas

Put the coconut cream and heavy cream in a bowl and whisk until thick but floppy.

Peel the bananas and toss in the lime juice and zest. Lightly oil a preheated stove top grill pan and cook the bananas, turning once, for 2–3 minutes, or until soft and browned.

Toast the dry unsweetened coconut on a piece of foil under a broiler until lightly browned. Serve the bananas with the coconut cream, sprinkled with the toasted coconut.

SERVES 6

2½ tbsp sago, soaked in water
   for at least 20 minutes

generous 1 cup warm water

scant 2 tbsp sugar

1 large, ripe mango, weighing about
   10 oz/280 g

generous ¾ cup heavy
   whipping cream

1 tbsp powdered gelatin, dissolved
   in generous 1 cup warm water

MONG GWO BOU DIN
mango dessert

Put the drained sago and warm water in a pan. Bring to a boil and then cook over low heat for 10 minutes, stirring frequently, until thick. Stir in the sugar and let cool.

Peel the mango and slice off the flesh from the pit. Reduce the mango to a smooth paste in a food processor or blender. Stir in the cream and then the gelatin.

Combine all the ingredients. Pour into 6 small bowls, cover with plastic wrap, and refrigerate until set.

VARIATION
Other soft, ripe fruits, such as peach, can be substituted if mango is not available.

SERVES 4–6

finely grated zest and juice of 1 lime

1 lb/450 g fresh fruit, such as bananas, guavas, oranges, kumquats, mangoes, melons, and pineapple

plain yogurt, to serve

SPICED SYRUP

1¼ cups superfine sugar

⅔ cup water

1 vanilla bean, sliced lengthwise, but left whole

1 cinnamon stick, broken in half

½ tsp fennel seeds

½ tsp black peppercorns, lightly crushed

½ tsp cumin seeds

PHAL KI CHAAT

spiced fruit salad

Begin by making the Spiced Syrup. Put the sugar, half the water, and the vanilla bean, cinnamon stick, fennel seeds, peppercorns, and cumin seeds into a small, heavy-bottomed pan over medium-high heat. Slowly bring to a boil, stirring to dissolve the sugar. As soon as the sugar boils, stop stirring and let the syrup bubble, until it turns golden brown.

Stand back from the pan and stir in the remaining water: take care because the syrup will splash and splatter. Stir again to dissolve any caramel, then remove the pan from the heat and let the syrup cool slightly.

Meanwhile, put the lime zest and juice in a large, heatproof bowl. Prepare and cut each fruit as required and add it to the bowl. If you are using bananas, toss them immediately in the lime juice to prevent discoloration.

Pour in the syrup and let the fruit and syrup cool completely, then cover the bowl with plastic wrap, and chill for at least 1 hour before serving with thick, creamy yogurt.

COOK'S TIP

If you are including oranges, pineapples, or any other juicy fruit, be sure to include the juice and squeeze the membranes and peels to extract extra juice. Work over the bowl when segmenting fruit so that you can catch the juices.

SERVES 4

4 medium-ripe pears

generous ¾ cup water

1 tsp sugar

1 tbsp honey

MAT JIN SYUT LEI
pears in honey syrup

Peel each pear, leaving the stalk intact. Wrap each in aluminum foil and place in a pan with the stalks resting on the side of the pan. Add enough water to cover at least half of the height of the pears. Bring to a boil and simmer for 30 minutes. Remove the pears and carefully take off the aluminum foil, reserving any juices. Set the pears aside to cool.

Bring the measured water to a boil in a pan. Add any pear juices, with the sugar and honey and boil for 5 minutes. Remove from the heat and let cool a little.

To serve, place each pear in a small individual dish. Pour a little syrup over each and serve just warm.

COOK'S TIP
Serve in small, dark-colored bowls to accentuate the color and shape of the pears.

SERVES 4

generous 1½ cups all-purpose flour

2 tbsp soft, light brown sugar

2 eggs

scant 2 cups milk

grated zest and juice of 1 lemon

4 tbsp unsalted butter

3 bananas

4 tbsp light corn syrup

PANG HO KHUAY
banana-stuffed crêpes

Combine the flour and sugar in a bowl, then beat in the eggs and half the milk. Beat together until smooth. Gradually add the remaining milk, stirring constantly, to make a smooth batter. Stir in the lemon zest.

Melt a little butter in an 8-inch/20-cm skillet and pour in one fourth of the batter. Tilt the pan to coat the bottom, and cook for 1–2 minutes, or until set. Flip the crêpe over and cook the second side. Slide it out of the pan and keep it warm. Repeat to make 3 more crêpes.

Slice the bananas and toss in the lemon juice. Pour the syrup over them and toss together. Fold each crêpe into 4 and fill the centers with the banana mixture. Serve warm.

SERVES 4

⅔ cup coconut cream

generous 1½ cups all-purpose flour

2 tbsp superfine sugar

2 eggs

scant 2 cups milk

⅔ cup coconut cream

⅓ cup dry unsweetened coconut

4 tbsp unsalted butter

½ melon, seeded, peeled, and
  thinly sliced, to serve

whipped cream, to serve

KANUM BUANG MA-PROW OON
mini coconut crêpes

Sift the flour in a bowl and stir in the sugar. Beat in the eggs and half the milk. Gradually beat in the remaining milk and then the coconut cream to make a creamy batter. Stir in the dry unsweetened coconut.

Melt a little of the butter in a heavy-bottomed skillet. Add 3–4 tablespoons of the batter, spacing them well apart because they will spread during cooking. Cook for 1–2 minutes, then flip over to cook the other sides. Remove from the pan and keep warm. Cook the remaining batter in the same way. Serve warm with melon slices and whipped cream.

SERVES 4–6

pinch of saffron threads

⅔ cup heavy cream, plus extra to serve

⅔ cup milk

generous 4 tbsp superfine sugar

seeds from 3 green cardamom pods

½ cinnamon stick

¼ cup finely chopped, dried mixed fruit,
   such as apricots, mangoes, and figs

6 tbsp ghee, vegetable oil, or peanut oil

6 slices of white bread, crusts removed
   and cut into triangles

freshly grated nutmeg, to decorate

chilled cream, to serve

SHAHI TUKDA
asian bread dessert

Put the saffron threads in a dry pan over high heat and "toast," stirring frequently, until you can smell the aroma. Immediately tip them out of the pan.

Put the cream, milk, sugar, cardamom seeds, cinnamon, and fruit in the pan over medium-high heat. Add the saffron threads and heat just until small bubbles appear around the edge, stirring to dissolve the sugar. Remove the pan from the heat and let the saffron infuse for at least 15 minutes.

Meanwhile, preheat the oven to 400°F/200°C and lightly grease a 10 x 7-inch/25 x 18-cm ovenproof serving dish.

Melt a third of the ghee in a large skillet over medium-high heat. Add as many bread triangles as will fit in a single layer and cook until golden brown, then turn over and repeat on the other sides. Remove from the pan and drain on some crumpled paper towels. Continue cooking all the bread triangles, adding more ghee as necessary.

Arrange the bread slices in the ovenproof dish and pour the cream and flavorings over the top. Remove the cinnamon stick. Bake for 20 minutes, or until the top is golden brown. Let stand for a few minutes, then lightly grate fresh nutmeg over the top. Serve hot with chilled cream for pouring over.

SERVES 6–8

1 tbsp peanuts

1 tbsp pine nuts

1 tbsp lotus seeds

8 oz/225 g mixed dried fruits (raisins,
   kumquats, prunes, dates, etc.)

scant 8½ cups water

generous ½ cup sugar

generous 1 cup glutinous rice, soaked in
   cold water for at least 2 hours

LAAP BAAT JUK
winter rice dessert with dried fruits

Soak the peanuts, pine nuts, and lotus seeds in a bowl of cold water for at least 1 hour. Soak the dried fruits as necessary. Chop all larger fruits into small pieces.

Bring the water to a boil in a large pan, add the sugar, and stir until dissolved. Drain the rice, nuts, lotus seeds, and mixed fruits, and add to the pan. Bring back to a boil. Cover and simmer over very low heat for 1 hour, stirring frequently. Serve warm.

COOK'S TIP
The texture of this dish should be that of a very thick soup. Simply add more water to create a slightly thinner version.

SERVES 4–6

scant ½ cup basmati rice

5 cups milk

seeds from 4 green cardamom pods

1 cinnamon stick

½ cup superfine sugar, or to taste

TO SERVE

grated jaggery or light brown
  sugar (optional)

chopped toasted pistachios (optional)

KHEER
luxury rice dessert

Rinse the basmati rice in several changes of water until the water runs clear, then let soak for 30 minutes. Drain and set aside until ready to cook.

Rinse a pan with cold water and do not dry. Pour the milk into the pan, add the cardamom seeds and cinnamon stick, and stir in the rice and superfine sugar.

Put the pan over medium-high heat and slowly bring to a boil, stirring. Reduce the heat to its lowest setting and let the mixture simmer, stirring frequently, for 1 hour, or until the rice is tender and the milky mixture has thickened. When the rice is tender, you can stir in extra milk if you would like a dessert with a soupier texture, or continue simmering if you prefer it thicker.

Spoon into individual bowls and sprinkle with jaggery to serve hot, or transfer to a bowl and let cool completely, stirring frequently. Cover with plastic wrap and chill until ready to serve. Spoon the dessert into individual bowls, and sprinkle with the pistachios, if using.

VARIATION
Transform this into a celebration dessert by decorating it with silver leaf.

SERVES 6–8

3½ cups water

⅛ oz/5 g agar-agar

generous 1 cup sugar

½ cup canned evaporated milk

1 tsp almond extract

GINGER SAUCE

3½ oz /100 g piece of fresh gingerroot,
  coarsely chopped

3½ cups water

generous 4 tbsp brown sugar

GEUNG JAP HANG YAN JE LEI

almond gelatin dessert in ginger sauce

To prepare the gelatin dessert, bring the water to a boil. Add the agar-agar and stir until dissolved. Stir in the sugar.

Pour through a strainer into a shallow dish. Pour in the evaporated milk, stirring constantly. When slightly cooled, stir in the almond extract. Chill in the refrigerator while you make the Ginger Sauce.

To make the Ginger Sauce, boil the gingerroot, water, and sugar in a covered pan for at least 1½ hours, or until the sauce is golden in color. Discard the gingerroot.

With a knife, cut thin slices of the gelatin dessert and arrange in individual bowls. Pour a little sauce, warm or cold, over the top.

VARIATION

The ginger sauce is also delicious served with soft bean curd.

SERVES 6–8

¾ cup coconut cream

2½ cups heavy cream

generous 1 cup confectioners' sugar

2 bananas

1 tsp lemon juice

¾ cup coconut cream

fresh fruit, to serve

I TIM MA-PROWN SAI KHUAY
banana and coconut ice cream

Whip the cream with the confectioners' sugar, until thick but still floppy. Mash the bananas with the lemon juice and whisk gently into the cream together with the coconut cream.

Transfer to a freezerproof container and freeze overnight. Serve in scoops with fresh fruit.

COOK'S TIP
Take care not to overwhip the cream, or it will curdle when the other ingredients are added.

SERVES 4

½ tsp saffron threads

5 tbsp milk

1 tbsp ground rice

½ tbsp ground almonds

scant 1 cup canned evaporated milk

scant 1 cup heavy cream

2 tbsp superfine sugar

few sprigs of fresh mint, to decorate

2 tbsp chopped blanched almonds,
  toasted, to serve

KESAR BADAAM KULFI

saffron and almond kulfi

Put the saffron threads in a dry skillet over high heat and "toast," stirring frequently, until you can smell the aroma, then tip them out of the pan.

Put the milk in the pan over medium-high heat, add the saffron, and heat until bubbles appear around the edge. Remove the pan from the heat and let the saffron infuse for at least 15 minutes. Meanwhile, combine the ground rice and almonds in a heatproof bowl. Put a flat, freezerproof container into the freezer.

Reheat the milk and saffron until bubbles appear around the edge, then slowly beat the saffron milk into the almond mixture, beating until it is smooth.

Pour the evaporated milk into a pan over medium-high heat and bring to a boil, stirring. Remove the pan from the heat and stir into the milk mixture. Stir in the cream and sugar. Return the pan to medium heat and simmer, stirring constantly, for 5–10 minutes, or until it thickens, but do not boil. Remove the pan from the heat and set aside, stirring frequently, to cool.

If using metal kulfi molds, put them in the freezer. Meanwhile, pour the saffron mixture into the freezerproof bowl and freeze for 30 minutes, then beat to break up any ice crystals. Beat every 30 minutes until the ice cream is almost firm.

Divide the mixture among 4 kulfi molds or ramekins. Cover with the lid or plastic wrap and freeze for at least 2 hours until solid. To serve, dip a cloth in hot water, wring it out, and rub it around the sides of the molds or ramekins, then invert onto plates. Decorate with fresh mint, sprinkle with the toasted almonds, and serve.

SERVES 4

generous 1 cup superfine sugar

2½ cups water

grated zest and juice of 2 limes

1 small pineapple, peeled, cut into
fourths, and chopped

sweet cookies, to serve

SUBPAROT, MA-NAU I TIM
pineapple and lime sherbet

Put the sugar and water into a pan and heat gently, stirring, until the sugar has dissolved. Bring to a boil and simmer for 10 minutes.

Stir in the grated zest and half the lime juice. Remove from the heat and let cool.

Put the pineapple in a blender or food processor and process until smooth. Add to the cold syrup with the remaining lime juice. Pour into a freezerproof container and freeze until crystals have formed around the edge.

Turn out the sherbet into a bowl. Beat well with a fork to break up any ice crystals. Return to the freezer and chill overnight. Serve in scoops with sweet cookies.

SERVES 4

scant 2 cups heavy cream

⅔ cup plain yogurt

4 tbsp ginger syrup (from the preserved
ginger jar)

6 pieces preserved ginger, chopped,
plus extra to decorate

4 tbsp soft brown sugar

4 oz/115 g phyllo pastry

4 tbsp unsalted butter, melted

3 tbsp sesame seeds

248

KA-NUM RUNG OB YHA RAD NA KHING

ginger creams and sesame pastries

Whip the cream until thick but not floppy. Stir in the yogurt and the ginger syrup. Divide the preserved ginger among 4 glasses or cups and then top with the ginger cream. Sprinkle 1 tablespoon of sugar over each one and chill overnight.

Preheat the oven to 400°F/200°C. Cut the phyllo into 16 squares measuring about 4 inches/ 10 cm. Brush 1 square with melted butter, then place another square on top. Repeat twice more to make 4 layers. Make 3 more piles of 4 layers in the same way.

Brush with butter and sprinkle with sesame seeds and bake for 10–15 minutes, or until golden brown. Decorate the ginger creams with pieces of preserved ginger and serve with the warm sesame phyllo.

MAKES 4–6 GLASSES

2½ oz/70 g fresh gingerroot, very finely chopped

½ tbsp finely grated lemon zest

5 cups boiling water

2 tbsp fresh lemon juice, or to taste

4 tbsp superfine sugar, or to taste

TO DECORATE

slices of fresh lemon

sprigs of fresh mint

ADRAK KA SHERBET

ginger cordial

Put the gingerroot in a heatproof bowl with the lemon zest. Pour over the boiling water, stir, and let steep overnight.

Strain the liquid into a large pitcher. Stir in the lemon juice and sugar, stirring until the sugar dissolves. Taste and add extra lemon juice and sugar, if desired. Serve in tall glasses decorated with lemon slices and sprigs of mint.

MAKES 4–6 GLASSES

1 large mango, ideally an Alphonso
   mango, coarsely chopped

scant 3 cups plain yogurt

generous 1 cup cold water

2 tbsp superfine sugar, or to taste

fresh lime juice, to taste

ice cubes

ground ginger, to decorate (optional)

252 AAM KI LASSI
mango lassi

Put 9 oz/250 g of the mango flesh in a food processor or blender with the yogurt and whizz until smooth (use any remaining mango for a fruit salad.) Add the water and whizz again to blend.

The amount of sugar you will add depends on how sweet the mango is. Stir in sugar to taste, then stir in the lime juice.

Fill 4 or 6 glasses with ice cubes and pour over the mango mixture. Lightly dust the top of each glass with ground ginger, if desired.

COOK'S TIP

When buying a fresh mango, look for an unblemished skin. A ripe mango will yield slightly when you squeeze it. You can also try to bring on an underripe mango by placing it with an apple in a plastic bag with a few holes poked through. The larger the mango, the greater the fruit-to-seed ratio will be. Take care when you cut the mango, because mango juice can stain.

Index